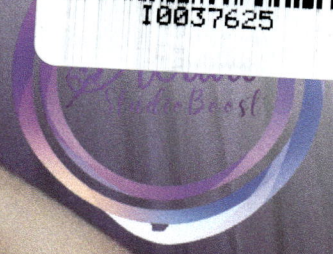
AERIAL

BUSINESS BLUEPRINT

How to Build, Grow, & Scale
Your Aerial Arts Studio

Contents

Introduction

From zero to 1000+ students: Learn the proven strategies behind a successful aerial arts studio. This isn't theory - it's a real-world blueprint from someone who's built, operated, and scaled an aerial arts academy from the ground up. Whether you're dreaming of opening your first studio or looking to grow your existing business, this book provides the exact framework, pricing strategies, and operational systems you need to succeed.

About the Author

NICOLA - AERIAL STUDIO BOOST OWNER & AERIAL ARTS ACADEMY FOUNDER

"I'm passionate about helping aerial arts studio owners build thriving businesses that truly serve their communities. My journey hasn't been a straight line - I've made mistakes, learned hard lessons, and discovered what really works through real-world experience.

My background spans over 20 years in marketing across diverse industries including fitness, automotive, health and safety, and education. This experience taught me that successful businesses are built on solid foundations, not just passion alone.

When I bought Dance Inspires, Oxford's first pole dance school, I thought I understood what I was getting into. The reality was much more challenging - venue problems, inherited operational issues, and financial pressures that eventually led to closure. But every setback taught me something valuable about business ownership.

In 2019, I decided to start fresh with Aerial Arts Academy. This time, I applied everything I'd learned - flexible venue partnerships instead of risky leases, systematic training programs, and scalable systems from day one. The difference was remarkable.

When COVID-19 hit in April 2020, I could have panicked. Instead, I saw an opportunity to innovate. Within weeks, we'd moved everything online and created the Aerial Education Hub. We didn't lose a single member during lockdown - in fact, it strengthened our community.

About the Author

NICOLA - AERIAL STUDIO BOOST OWNER & AERIAL ARTS ACADEMY FOUNDER

What I've learned is that taking care of your team is the foundation of everything else. At Aerial Arts Academy, our instructors receive comprehensive support - mental and financial assistance for certifications, dedicated training time, competitive pay, and flexible scheduling. When your team thrives, your students thrive, and your business thrives.

Today, Aerial Arts Academy serves over 1000 students across multiple venues. We're planning franchise development because I believe the systems we've created can help other communities access quality aerial arts instruction.

Through Aerial Studio Boost, I share the real strategies that have worked for me - not theory, but practical systems tested in the real world. I believe in being transparent about both successes and failures because that's how we all learn and grow.

> **My mission is simple:**
> To help new or existing studio owners avoid the mistakes I made and build sustainable businesses that transform lives through aerial arts. Every expert was once a beginner, and I'm here to help you on that journey.

PART 1: FOUNDATION (Chapters 1-4)

→

Chapter 1

THE AERIAL ARTS OPPORTUNITY

Five years ago, I had a dream and very little in savings. Today, I run a thriving aerial arts academy with 1000+ students across multiple venues, a large team of specialised instructors, and franchise opportunities on the horizon. I'm also the founder of Aerial Studio Boost, a platform dedicated to helping aerial studio owners scale their businesses. This isn't luck - it's a blueprint you can follow."

My name is Nicola, and I'm the owner and founder of Aerial Arts Academy, one of the UK's fastest-growing aerial arts businesses. But my journey didn't start in a boardroom or with a business degree - it started with a single pole class that changed my life.

Like many of you reading this, I fell in love with aerial arts as a student first. The feeling of defying gravity, the supportive community, the way it challenged both my body and mind - I knew I had found something special. But what started as personal passion quickly evolved into something bigger when I realised the incredible business opportunity in front of me.

Chapter 1

THE AERIAL ARTS OPPORTUNITY

From Student to Multi-Venue Owner

Here's the thing - Aerial Arts Academy wasn't actually my first rodeo in the studio business. Back in 2013, I aquired Dance Inspires alongside a business partner. It was Oxford's very first pole dance school. For six years, I practically built that business from the ground up, navigating all the challenges of being a pioneer in a market that barely understood what pole / aerial was about.

When I sold Dance Inspires in early 2019 I thought I might be done with the studio world. But you know what they say about entrepreneurs... we can't help ourselves!

I launched Aerial Arts Academy in November 2019, right as the world was about to change forever. Just five months later, in April 2021, we were forced to shut our doors due to lockdown restrictions. But here's where the real test of leadership comes in - I had members who believed in what we were building, and I wasn't about to let them down.

So I did what any determined entrepreneur would do: I pivoted. Fast. Within days, I moved our entire operation online via Zoom. But this wasn't just a temporary fix - I created something that would become one of our greatest assets: the Aerial Education Hub. This comprehensive online platform houses our complete syllabus and class content, giving members access to professional aerial training from anywhere.

The result? I didn't lose a single member during lockdown.
Not one.

Chapter 1

THE AERIAL ARTS OPPORTUNITY

That experience taught me that business isn't just about having a great product - it's about showing up for your community when it matters most. To this day, every single member gets free access to the Aerial Education Hub as my forever thank you for staying with us through the uncertainty.

That's how Aerial Arts Academy was truly born - not just as another fitness studio, but as a business built on unshakeable loyalty and innovation under pressure.

Within 12 months, we had waiting lists for classes and were expanding to multiple venues. Today, Aerial Arts Academy operates across several locations with over 1000 active students and a team of specialised instructors. We serve everyone from 8-year-olds in our youth programs to adults discovering their strength for the first time.

But the real transformation happened when I realised that my success wasn't just about running one great studio - it was about creating a system that could help other passionate instructors and entrepreneurs build their own thriving aerial arts businesses.

Chapter 1

THE AERIAL ARTS OPPORTUNITY

The Birth of Aerial Studio Boost

That realisation led me to create Aerial Studio Boost, a comprehensive platform designed specifically for aerial studio owners who want to scale their businesses. Through Aerial Studio Boost, I aim to help studio owners implement the same systems, strategies, and frameworks that took Aerial Arts Academy from a single-venue startup to a multi-location operation.

What Makes My Approach Different?

Here's what sets me apart from other business coaches or consultants in the fitness space:

→ **Real-World Experience:**

I'm not teaching theory - I'm sharing systems that currently generate revenue across multiple venues with 1000+ students.

→ **Industry Specialisation:**

I don't work with generic fitness businesses. I specialise exclusively in aerial arts studios because I understand the unique challenges, opportunities, and operational requirements.

→ **Proven Scale:**

Most aerial studio owners struggle to break past 100 students. I've built systems that support 1000+ students across multiple venues while maintaining quality and community.

→ **Complete Business Integration:**

Through Aerial Studio Boost, I help with everything from marketing and operations to team management and financial planning—not just one piece of the puzzle.

Access your free subscripton to Aerial Studio Boost online for free resources

"Every studio owner I work with becomes part of a larger movement. We're not just building businesses; we're creating spaces where people discover their strength, build confidence, and find community in an increasingly disconnected world."

Nicola Ghalmi,
Aerial Studio Boost Founder

Chapter 1

THE AERIAL ARTS OPPORTUNITY

The Fitness Revolution is Here

Walk into any gym today and you'll see the same thing: rows of treadmills, weight machines, and people going through the motions. But step into an aerial arts studio, and everything changes. Students are laughing, challenging themselves in ways they never imagined, and building genuine community around shared achievement.

The aerial arts industry isn't just growing - it's exploding. What started as a niche skill derived from circus on the aerials, and strippers and sex workers on the pole side, has evolved into one of the fastest-growing fitness trends globally. And if you're reading this book, you're perfectly positioned to capitalise on this opportunity... (respecting its originators and origins of course!).

Why Now is Your Moment

The numbers don't lie. The global aerial fitness market is projected to reach £1.2 billion by 2027, growing at a compound annual growth rate of 8.5%. But here's what those statistics don't tell you: this growth is happening in communities everywhere, not just major cities.

When I opened Aerial Arts Academy in Oxfordshire, I wasn't in London or Manchester. I was in a university town where people told me "aerial arts won't work here any more." They were wrong. Within 12 months, we had waiting lists for classes and were expanding to multiple venues. Today, we operate across several locations with over 1000 active students and a team of 23+ specialised instructors.

Chapter 1

THE AERIAL ARTS OPPORTUNITY

The Perfect Storm of Opportunity

Several factors are converging to create unprecedented opportunity in the aerial arts space:

1. Post-Pandemic Fitness Shift

People are craving experiences, not just exercise. After years of home workouts and isolation, they want community, challenge, and something that makes them feel alive. Aerial arts delivers all three.

2. Social Media Amplification

Instagram and TikTok have made aerial arts incredibly shareable. Every student becomes a walking advertisement when they post their progress videos. With 1000+ students, that's 1000+ potential brand ambassadors creating organic content daily.

3. Demographic Expansion

Aerial arts is no longer just for young, flexible women. Across our venues, I've taught everyone from 8-year-olds to 65-year-olds, from complete beginners to former gymnasts. The market is broader than most people realise. Everyone regardless of gender, race or religious background, is welcome.

4. Limited Competition

In most markets, there are still only 1-2 established aerial studios, if any. Compare this to yoga studios or traditional gyms, where saturation is common. You're entering a blue ocean with room for massive expansion.

Chapter 1

What Makes Aerial Arts Studios Different

Having run both traditional fitness programs and aerial arts classes across multiple venues, I can tell you the difference is night and day:

Traditional Fitness:
- High churn rates (average 30% annually)
- Price-sensitive customers
- Limited community building
- Difficult to differentiate

Aerial Arts:
- High retention (our average student stays 18+ months)
- Value-conscious customers who invest in experiences
- Natural community building around shared challenges
- Unique offering that's hard to replicate

The Numbers That Matter

Let me share some real data from Aerial Arts Academy to show you what's possible at scale:

- Total active students: 1000+ across all venues
- Average class size: 8-15 students (we cap at 15 for safety)
- Class price: £15 pay-as-you-go
- Member retention: 85% year-over-year
- Revenue per member: £65-149 monthly (depending on membership tier)
- Team size: 23+ specialised instructors
- Instructor costs: £15-45 per hour (experience dependent)
- Venue costs: 30-40% of revenue (varies by location)
- Multiple revenue streams: Classes, privates, parties, workshops, youth programs, and events

Chapter 1

THE AERIAL ARTS OPPORTUNITY

Your Ideal Customer is Waiting

One of the biggest mistakes new studio owners make is trying to appeal to everyone. After years of running classes across multiple venues and serving 1000+ students, I can tell you exactly who your ideal customer is:

Primary Demographics:

→ Age: 18-45 (though we serve 8-no age limit, across all programs, being in a University town means that we attract a younger demographic)

→ Income: Any class

→ Lifestyle: Values experiences over possessions

→ Fitness level: Beginner through to advanced

Psychographics:

→ Seeks community and belonging

→ Wants to challenge themselves in new ways

→ Values personal growth and achievement

→ Willing to invest in quality instruction

What They're Really Buying:

→ Confidence and empowerment

→ A supportive community

→ Stress relief and mental health benefits

→ A unique skill they can be proud of

→ An escape from daily routine

Chapter 1

THE AERIAL ARTS OPPORTUNITY

The Business Model That Works at Scale

Here's what most people don't understand about aerial arts studios: they're not just fitness businesses - they're community businesses with recurring revenue models that can scale exponentially.

Revenue Streams Across Multiple Venues:

1. Membership subscriptions (70% of revenue)
2. Pay-as-you-go classes (15% of revenue)
3. Private lessons (8% of revenue)
4. Workshops and events (5% of revenue)
5. Retail and merchandise (2% of revenue)

This diversification creates stability that single-revenue fitness businesses can't match. When you multiply this across multiple venues with 1000+ students, you create a business with serious scale and impact.

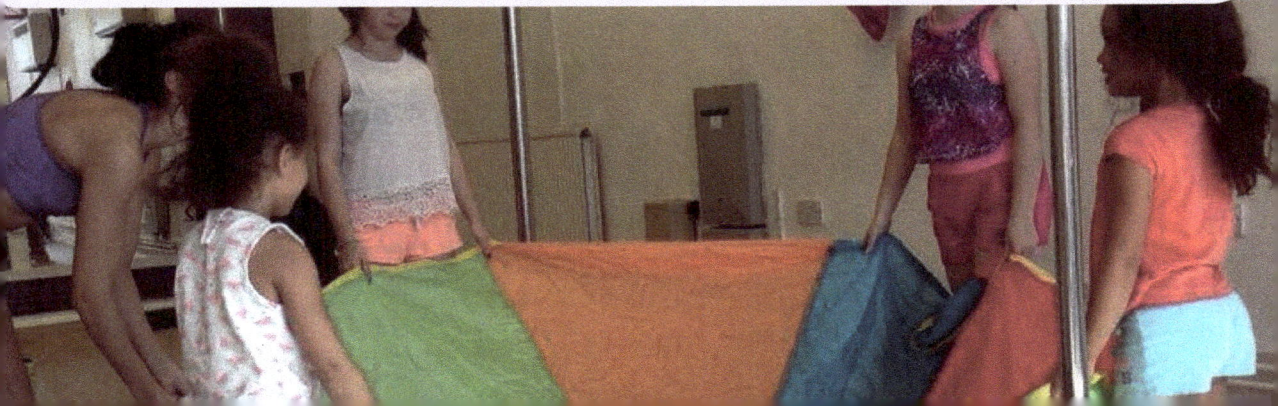

Chapter 1

THE AERIAL ARTS OPPORTUNITY

The Multi-Venue Advantage

Operating across multiple venues has taught me invaluable lessons about scaling:

Benefits of Multi-Venue Operations:

- <u>Risk Distribution:</u> One venue's slow month doesn't sink the business

- <u>Economies of Scale:</u> Bulk equipment purchases, shared marketing costs

- <u>Team Development:</u> Career progression paths for instructors

- <u>Market Domination:</u> Become the go-to aerial arts provider in your region

- <u>Franchise Preparation:</u> Perfect testing ground for replicable systems

Managing a Large Team

With 23+ instructors across multiple venues, I've learned that success isn't just about finding good teachers - it's about creating systems that allow great instructors to thrive while maintaining consistency across all locations.

The Challenges (And Why They're Opportunities)

I won't sugarcoat it - running a multi-venue aerial arts operation with 1000+ students has unique challenges:

- Safety Requirements: Higher insurance costs and strict safety protocols across all venues
- Equipment Investment: Initial setup costs multiply with each location
- Instructor Training: Specialised skills require ongoing education and consistent standards
- Venue Limitations: Not every space works for aerial arts
- Team Management: Coordinating schedules and maintaining culture across locations

But here's the thing: these challenges are exactly what create your competitive moat. They're barriers to entry that protect your business once you're established, and they become easier to manage with proven systems.

Chapter 1

THE AERIAL ARTS OPPORTUNITY

What This Book Will Give You

Over the next chapters, I'm going to share everything I've learned building Aerial Arts Academy from a dream to a multi-venue operation serving 1000+ students, plus the systems I've developed through Aeial Studio Boost to help other studio owners achieve similar success:

→ The exact financial models and pricing strategies that work at scale

→ How to find, train, and retain a large team of exceptional instructors

→ Marketing systems that fill classes consistently across multiple venues

→ Leadership principles for building strong team culture at scale

→ Operational systems that support rapid growth

→ Multi-venue management strategies and franchise preparation

→ Real case studies from my journey (including the mistakes)

This isn't theory - it's a proven blueprint from someone who's scaled it and helped others do the same.

Your Journey Starts Now

In the following chapter, we'll dive into the foundational elements you need to get started - from legal structure to initial investment planning for single and multi-venue operations. But first, take a moment to envision your own aerial arts studio. What would it look like? Who would you serve? What impact would you create?
Are you ready to build something extraordinary?

Your blueprint starts here...

Chapter 2

YOUR BUSINESS BLUEPRINT

The difference between a dream and a business is a plan. The difference between a plan and success is execution. In this chapter, I'll give you the exact blueprint I used to build Aerial Arts Academy into a multi-venue operation serving 1000+ students. By the end of this chapter, you'll be filling out your own Blue Print Action Plan before we delve into more specific business areas and deeper plans for those.

The Foundation That Everything Builds On

When I launched Aerial Arts Academy in November 2019, I didn't just wing it. I had already learned from building and selling Dance Inspires that success in the studio business requires solid foundations from day one. The legal structure, financial planning, and operational framework you establish at the beginning will either support your growth or limit it.

Let me walk you through the exact blueprint I used - and the lessons I learned the hard way the first time around.

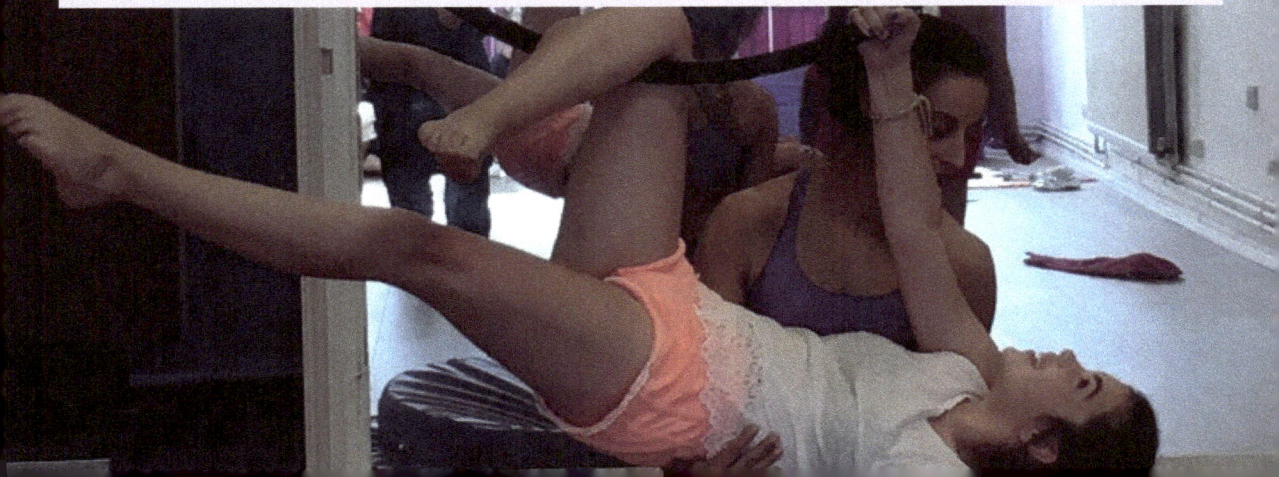

Chapter 2

YOUR BUSINESS BLUEPRINT

Legal Structure: Getting It Right From Day One

Choose Your Business Structure Wisely
Your legal structure affects everything from taxes to liability to how you can raise capital for expansion. Here's what I recommend based on my experience.

When I started Aerial Arts Academy, I chose to operate as a sole trader for several practical reasons:

→ Simpler setup and accounting

→ Direct control over all business decisions

→ Lower administrative burden

→ All profits are personal income

→ Easier to manage initially when building the business

What I Did:

I structured Aerial Arts Academy as a sole trader from launch. This gave me the flexibility I needed during our rapid growth phase and simplified the financial management when we had to pivot during lockdown. As a sole trader, I could make quick decisions and adapt our business model without complex corporate procedures.

Limited Company (Consider for Future Growth)

As your business scales, you might want to consider converting to a limited company for:

- Personal liability protection
- Tax efficiency for reinvestment
- Professional credibility with larger venues and suppliers
- Easier to bring in investors or partners later
- Clean structure for eventual sale or franchising

The Reality:
Many successful studio owners operate as sole traders throughout their entire journey. I find it works wonders this way for me. The key is understanding the implications and planning accordingly.

Chapter 2

YOUR BUSINESS BLUEPRINT

Insurance: Your Safety Net

As a sole trader, comprehensive insurance becomes even more critical because you have unlimited personal liability. Here's your essential coverage:

Public Liability Insurance

- Minimum £2 million coverage (I recommend £5 million)
- Covers student injuries during classes
- Required by most venue rental agreements
- Absolutely essential as a sole trader
  - this protects your personal assets

Professional Indemnity Insurance

- Covers claims against your teaching methods
- Essential if you're creating training
- programs

Access your free subscripton to Aerial Studio Boost online for free resources

Equipment Insurance

- Covers theft, damage, and replacement
- Include rigging points and safety equipment

Personal Income Protection

- Covers your income if you're unable to work due to injury
- Particularly important for sole traders with no employer benefits

My Insurance Recommendation: Insure4Sport (https://www.insure4sport.co.uk) After years of dealing with various insurance providers, I highly recommend Insure4Sport for aerial arts businesses, especially sole traders. As a sole trader, I've found Insure4Sport's understanding of our industry invaluable. They know exactly what coverage we need and don't try to sell unnecessary add-ons.

Why This Matters: A Cautionary Tale

Imagine this scenario: A student attempts an advanced move they're not ready for and falls, claiming the instructor didn't provide adequate safety instruction. Without proper professional indemnity insurance, a sole trader could face personal liability for damages, legal fees, and compensation claims that could reach tens of thousands of pounds. This is exactly why comprehensive coverage isn't optional in our industry - it's the foundation of responsible business operation.

Chapter 2

YOUR BUSINESS BLUEPRINT

Location Strategy: Where Success Happens

Your venue choice can make or break your business. After operating across multiple locations, here's what I've learned:

→ Ceiling Height: Minimum 4m (13 feet) for aerial work

→ Structural Integrity: Engineered rigging points or beam capacity

→ Floor Space: 3x3 meters per aerial point minimum

→ Mirrors: Full-length mirrors on at least one wall

→ Climate Control: Air conditioning for student comfort

→ Parking: Accessible parking for evening and daytime classes

→ Changing Facilities: Clean, private changing areas

Location Types That Work:

1. Gym / Leisure Centre Partnerships (My Preferred Model)
   - Established customer base
   - Shared overhead costs
   - Professional facilities
   - Built-in marketing opportunities

Example: Our partnership with Feel Fit Gym provides us with premium facilities while giving them unique class offerings that differentiate them from competitors.

2. Dance Studios
   - Appropriate flooring and mirrors
   - Existing aerial-friendly infrastructure
   - Shared target demographic
   - Flexible rental arrangements

3. Dedicated Aerial Studios
   - Complete control over the environment
   - Higher overhead but higher profit margins
   - Ability to customise everything

23

Location Scouting Checklist:

☐ Ceiling height measured and verified

☐ Structural engineer assessment completed

☐ Insurance requirements confirmed with the venue

☐ Parking availability assessed

☐ Public transport accessibility checked

☐ Demographics of the surrounding area analysed

☐ Competition within a 3-mile radius mapped

☐ Rental terms negotiated (try for revenue share vs. fixed rent)

Chapter 2

YOUR BUSINESS BLUEPRINT

Operational Systems: The Backbone of Scale

The systems you build from day one determine whether you can scale beyond yourself. Here's what I implemented:

Booking and Payment System

We use Go Team Up, which integrates:

→ Online class booking

→ Automatic payment processing

→ Membership management

→ Waitlist management

→ Reporting and analytics

Class Management System:

- Maximum 15 students per class (safety and quality)
- 60-minute class duration (optimal for learning and scheduling)
- Progressive skill levels with clear advancement criteria
- Consistent class structure across all venues

Safety Protocols:

- Pre-class safety briefing (standardised script)
- Equipment inspection checklist
- Incident reporting system
- Regular equipment maintenance schedule
- Instructor safety certification requirements

Customer Communication:

- Welcome sequence for new students
- Regular newsletter with tips and updates
- Social media content calendar
- Feedback collection system
- Retention outreach for lapsed members

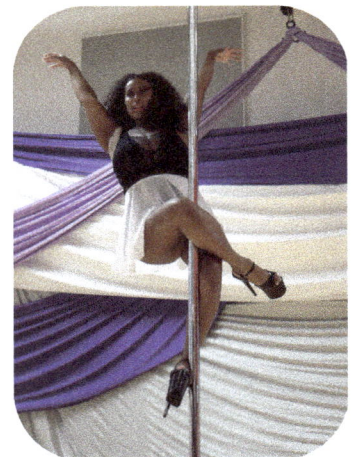

Chapter 2

YOUR BUSINESS BLUEPRINT

The Technology Stack That Scales

Essential Software:

→ **Booking System:** Go Team Up (£50-100/month scales with the number of active students you have)

→ **Website:** WordPress with booking integration

→ **Email Marketing:** Brevo, Hubspot or Mailchimp

→ **Social Media:** Social Pilot or Hootsuite for scheduling

→ **Accounting:** Xero or QuickBooks (essential for sole trader tax management)

→ **Communication:** Teams, Slack and / or WhatsApp for business for team coordination

The Aerial Education Hub

One of our biggest key differentiators is our online learning platform, born from necessity during lockdown. We will delve into this more later, but for now, it includes:

- Complete syllabus for all levels
- Video tutorials and progressions
- Home practice routines
- Flexibility and strength training
- Exclusive member content

This platform now serves as both a retention tool and an additional revenue stream, while providing value that no competitor can easily replicate.

Chapter 2

YOUR BUSINESS BLUEPRINT

Quality Control: Maintaining Standards Across Venues

As you scale, maintaining consistent quality becomes your biggest challenge. Here's how we do it:

Instructor Standards:

→ Minimum qualification requirements

→ Ongoing training and assessment

→ Standardised teaching methods

→ Regular performance reviews

→ Clear advancement pathways

Class Consistency:

→ Standardised warm-up and cool-down routines

→ Progressive skill development across all levels

→ Consistent safety protocols

→ Regular quality audits

→ Student feedback integration

Brand Standards:

→ Consistent visual identity across all venues

→ Standardised communication style

→ Uniform instructor presentation

→ Consistent pricing and policies

→ Regular brand compliance checks

Chapter 2

YOUR BUSINESS BLUEPRINT

Risk Management: Protecting Your Investment (Sole Trader Focus)

As a sole trader, risk management becomes particularly critical because your personal assets are directly at stake. Unlike limited companies, there's no corporate veil protecting your personal wealth, making comprehensive risk planning essential for long-term success.

Operational Risks and Solutions

The most immediate operational risk facing aerial studios is key instructor dependency. When your business relies heavily on one or two star instructors, their illness, departure, or unavailability can devastate your schedule. The solution lies in cross-training multiple instructors across different disciplines and maintaining a pool of qualified backup teachers who can step in when needed.

Equipment failure presents another significant operational challenge. Aerial equipment is subject to wear and stress, and unexpected failures can force class cancellations and create safety concerns. Maintaining backup equipment for critical items like poles, rigging points, and safety mats ensures continuity of operations while protecting your reputation for reliability.

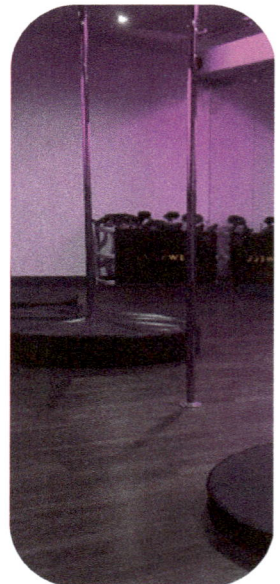

Venue loss represents perhaps the most serious operational risk, as we learned from the Dance Inspires experience. Relying on a single location creates vulnerability to landlord disputes, rent increases, or property changes. Diversifying across multiple venues not only spreads this risk but also provides opportunities for growth and market expansion.

Seasonal fluctuations affect most fitness businesses, with predictable drops during holidays and summer months. Developing strong retention strategies, offering flexible membership options, and creating year-round programming helps smooth these natural variations in attendance.

Chapter 2

YOUR BUSINESS BLUEPRINT

Financial Risk Management

Cash flow management forms the foundation of financial stability for sole traders. Maintaining three to six months of operating expenses in reserve provides the buffer needed to weather unexpected challenges or seasonal downturns. This reserve also enables you to take advantage of growth opportunities without compromising day-to-day operations.

Bad debt can quickly erode profitability in a membership-based business. Requiring payment in advance through automated billing systems eliminates most collection issues while improving cash flow predictability. The Go Team Up platform's integration with GoCardless and PayPal makes this process seamless for both studios and students.

Economic downturns test every business model, but those with diverse offerings tend to weather storms better. Developing online class options, digital content, and alternative revenue streams creates resilience against broader economic challenges. The Aerial Education Hub exemplifies this approach, providing value to members even when physical attendance isn't possible.

Competition is inevitable as the aerial arts industry grows, but studios that focus on community building and quality instruction create sustainable competitive advantages. Price competition rarely leads to long-term success, while exceptional student experiences and strong community connections build lasting loyalty.

Personal liability represents the most serious financial risk for sole traders. Comprehensive insurance coverage through specialists like Insure4Sport provides essential protection against claims that could otherwise threaten your personal assets and business survival.

Legal Risk Mitigation:

Legal risks in the aerial arts industry require proactive management rather than reactive responses. Comprehensive waivers and clear terms of service form the first line of defense, but these documents must be regularly reviewed and updated to reflect current legal standards and industry best practices.

Chapter 2

YOUR BUSINESS BLUEPRINT

Proper instructor classification remains a complex area where many studios face challenges. Understanding the distinction between employees and self-employed contractors is crucial, as misclassification can result in significant penalties and back-payments. When in doubt, seek professional advice rather than risking costly mistakes.

Compliance with health and safety regulations isn't optional in the aerial arts industry. Regular equipment inspections, proper instructor training, and documented safety procedures protect both students and your business. The investment in proper safety protocols is minimal compared to the potential costs of accidents or regulatory violations.

The key to effective risk management lies in viewing it as an investment in your business's future rather than an unnecessary expense. Each risk mitigation strategy should be evaluated based on its potential impact and the cost of implementation, with priority given to those risks that could threaten business survival.

Chapter 2

The Pivot Strategy: Lessons from Lockdown

When we were forced to close in April 2020, our survival depended on systems we'd built from day one. Here's what saved us:

→ **Digital Infrastructure:**
Our booking system and customer database allowed us to communicate instantly with all members.

→ **Community Focus:**
Because we'd built genuine relationships, members wanted to support us through the crisis.

→ **Adaptability:**
Our systematic approach to class delivery translated well to online formats.

→ **Innovation Mindset:**
We saw opportunity in crisis and created the Aerial Education Hub.

The result?

We didn't lose a single member and emerged stronger than before.

Access your free subscripton to Aerial Studio Boost online for free resources

Chapter 2

Your Blueprint Action Plan

Week 1-2: Legal Foundation
- ☐ Register as sole trader or LTD with HMRC
- ☐ Obtain necessary insurance coverage (contact Insure4Sport)
- ☐ Set up business banking and accounting systems
- ☐ Consult with the accountant on tax obligations and record-keeping

Week 3-4: Location and Setup
- ☐ Secure venue agreement
- ☐ Complete structural engineering assessment
- ☐ Install rigging points and equipment
- ☐ Set up booking and payment systems

Week 5-6: Operational Systems
- ☐ Develop safety protocols and procedures
- ☐ Create class curricula and progression systems
- ☐ Establish instructor hiring and training processes
- ☐ Launch marketing and pre-sales campaign

Week 7-8: Launch Preparation
- ☐ Conduct soft launch with friends and family
- ☐ Refine systems based on feedback
- ☐ Train the initial instructor team
- ☐ Prepare grand opening marketing campaign

Chapter 2

The Foundation for Everything That Follows

Your business blueprint isn't just about getting started - it's about building something that can grow. Every system you implement, every process you document, and every standard you establish becomes part of the foundation that will support your expansion to multiple venues and beyond.

Remember: The goal isn't just to open a studio - it's to build a business that can thrive, scale, and run with you leading a team. That starts with getting your blueprint right from day one, regardless of your business structure.

Conclusion

In the next chapter, we'll dive deep into venue mastery - how to find, evaluate, and secure the perfect locations for your aerial arts academy. But first, make sure you have your blueprint solid. Everything else builds on this foundation.

Chapter 3

VENUE MASTERY

"Your venue isn't just where you teach - it's where transformation happens. The right space can elevate your business from good to extraordinary, while the wrong one can kill even the best program. Here's how to find, evaluate, and secure venues that set you up for success." - Nicola

The Venue That Changed Everything - And The Nightmare That Taught Me

When I owned Dance Inspires in 2013, I did what most new business owners do - I took on a traditional lease. It was already in place, and I thought having "my own space" was the mark of a serious business. That lease became one of the most expensive lessons of my entrepreneurial journey.

The roof leaked constantly. I was always in "flea mode" - jumping from crisis to crisis, dealing with water damage, trying to reach an increasingly absent landlord. The building was in constant disrepair, and I was powerless to fix the fundamental problems because I didn't own the property. Eventually, the landlord served notice and converted the space into flats. Desperate to keep the business running, I started searching for a new location. I almost signed for an industrial unit - thank goodness I didn't! Imagine having that financial burden during lockdown when we were forced to close for months.

Instead, I made the smartest decision of my business career: I established partnerships with Oxford Academy and Feel Fit Gym. When I sold Dance Inspires in 2019 (and the new owner subsequently closed it), I already had those connections. When I started Aerial Arts Academy, I not only had established relationships but found an even better room at Oxford Academy with the perfect ceiling height to add aerial hoop and silks to our offerings. That experience taught me that venue ownership isn't about control - it's about finding the right partnerships that allow your business to thrive.

Chapter 3
VENUE MASTERY

Why Hourly Rental is Your Secret Weapon:

Let me be blunt: most new studio owners fail because they commit to expensive long-term leases before they've proven demand.
In expensive markets like Oxford, this is business suicide.

Here's why hourly rental transformed my business:

Financial Flexibility:

→ Started with 2-3 classes p/w, scaled up as demand grew

→ We had no massive upfront deposits or monthly lease commitments

→ Our costs scaled directly with revenue

→ We tested multiple venues simultaneously

Market Testing:

→ Tried different locations to find the ideal demographic

→ Tested various class times without long-term commitments

→ Had the option to pivot quickly if a venue didn't work

→ Built relationships with venue owners gradually

Access your free subscripton to Aerial Studio Boost online for free resources

Chapter 3
VENUE MASTERY

Risk Mitigation:

→ No personal guarantees on long-term leases

→ Can weather economic downturns more easily (crucial during lockdown)

→ Multiple venues mean you're not dependent on one location

→ Easy to add or drop venues based on performance

Growth Enablement:

→ Scale to multiple venues faster

→ Reinvest savings into equipment and marketing instead of rent

→ Build proof of concept before committing to permanent spaces

→ Create negotiating power for better long-term deals later

Access your free subscripton to Aerial Studio Boost online for free resources

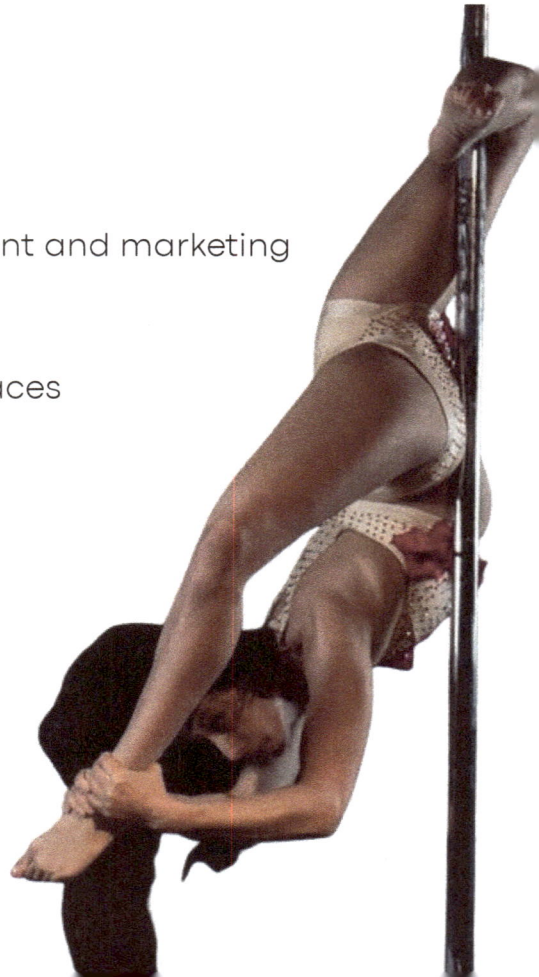

Chapter 3
VENUE MASTERY

The Venue Evaluation Framework

After evaluating dozens of potential venues and learning from my Dance Inspires experience, I've developed a systematic approach that saves time and prevents costly mistakes:

Physical Requirements (Non-Negotiable)

Ceiling Height: The Make-or-Break Factor
- Minimum 4 meters (13 feet) for basic aerial hoop/silks work
- 6+ meters ideal for aerial silks and advanced moves
- Measure from floor to lowest obstruction
- Account for rigging hardware (adds 30cm minimum)
- Check for ceiling fans, lights, or beams that reduce usable height.

This is why the Oxford Academy room was perfect - the ceiling height allowed us to expand from just hoops to include silks, dramatically increasing our class offerings.

Structural Integrity
- Exposed structural beams (like i-beams) are ideal for rigging
- Concrete ceilings require professional assessment
- Avoid suspended ceilings or false ceilings (unless there are i beams underneath!)
- Get structural engineer report if in doubt
- Learn from my Dance Inspires experience - building quality matters

Floor Space
- Minimum 3x3 meters per aerial point
- Allow for student movement and safety
- Consider equipment storage space
- Account for instructor demonstration area

Flooring
- Sprung wooden floors are ideal
- Avoid concrete (too hard for falls... although you should be using mats obviously!)
- Carpet is acceptable with proper mats (unless you have floor based classes, then this probably isn't ideal)
- Ensure level surface throughout

Chapter 3
VENUE MASTERY

Practical Considerations

Mirrors
- Full-length mirrors on at least one wall
- Essential for student safety and progress
- Check for cracks or distortion
- Consider portable mirrors if venue lacks them

Climate Control
- Air conditioning is essential (aerial work is intense)
- Heating for winter months
- Ventilation to prevent stuffiness
- Temperature control affects student comfort and retention

Changing Facilities
- Private changing areas / accessible toilet changing
- Clean, well-maintained facilities
- Adequate space for students to prepare
- Storage for personal belongings (and for your kit!)

Parking and Access
- Evening class parking is crucial
- Consider public transport links
- Wheelchair accessibility
- Safe, well-lit entrance

Chapter 3

VENUE MASTERY

Venue Types That Work

1. Gym Partnerships (My Preferred Model)
Why They Work:

→ Established customer base interested in fitness

→ Professional facilities and equipment

→ Shared marketing opportunities

→ Often have suitable spaces during off-peak hours

→ Professional management (unlike my Dance Inspires landlord experience)

What to Look For:

- Group exercise studios with high ceilings
- Gyms looking to diversify their offerings
- Established businesses with good reputations
- Flexible management willing to try new things

Negotiation Tips:

- Offer to promote their gym to your students
- Start with trial period to prove concept
- Provide insurance certificates upfront
- Offer gym members discounted rates

www.feelfitgym.com

Example: Our Feel Fit Gym Partnership
This partnership has been transformational for both businesses. They get unique classes that differentiate them from competitors, while we get access to premium facilities and their existing customer base. It's a true win-win relationship that's lasted through multiple business iterations.

Chapter 3
VENUE MASTERY

Venue Types That Work

2. Educational Partnerships
Why They Work:

→   Often have suitable spaces with high ceilings

→   Understand the needs of structured learning

→   Professional environment and management

→   Flexible scheduling around their primary activities

What to Look For:
- Dance studios or drama schools with appropriate spaces
- Educational institutions with suitable facilities
- Professional management and clear policies
- Complementary scheduling opportunities

Example: Our Oxford Academy Venue

The Oxford Academy has been instrumental in our success. When I transitioned from Dance Inspires to Aerial Arts Academy, not only did I maintain this relationship, but I found an even better room with the perfect ceiling height for aerial hoop and silks. This partnership demonstrates how venue relationships can evolve and improve over time.

Chapter 3

VENUE MASTERY

Venue Types That Work

3. Leisure Centres
Why They Work:

→   Affordable hourly rates

→   Good parking and accessibility

→   Often have changing facilities

→   Great footfall with a wide demographic range

What to Look For:

- Studio rooms with sufficient ceiling height
- Reliable booking systems
- Good community reputation
- Flexible management

Potential Challenges:

- Limited availability during peak times
- May require additional insurance

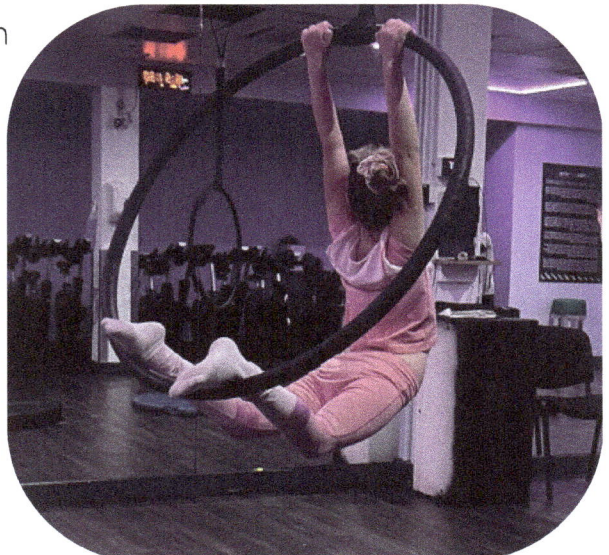

Chapter 3

VENUE MASTERY

The Venue Scouting Process

Step 1: Initial Research
- Map potential venues within your target area
- Research online for ceiling heights and facilities
- Check social media for photos and reviews
- Note contact information and availability
- Learn from others' experiences (avoid my Dance Inspires mistakes)

Step 2: Initial Contact
- Explain your business concept clearly
- Emphasise safety and professionalism
- Provide insurance certificates
- Request venue viewing
- Ask about management responsiveness and maintenance policies

Step 3: Physical Evaluation
- Measure ceiling height accurately
- Test structural integrity (where possible)
- Assess lighting and ventilation
- Check changing facilities and parking
- Evaluate overall building condition and maintenance

Step 4: Business Evaluation
- Discuss pricing and availability
- Understand cancellation policies
- Review insurance requirements
- Assess management flexibility and responsiveness
- Check references from other renters if possible

Step 5: Trial Period
- Negotiate short-term trial arrangement
- Test venue with actual classes
- Gather student feedback
- Evaluate business performance
- Assess management support and communication

Chapter 3

VENUE MASTERY

Negotiation Strategies That Work

Building Relationships

The key to successful venue partnerships lies in approaching venue owners as potential business partners rather than traditional landlords. This mindset shift changes the entire dynamic of your negotiations and creates opportunities for mutually beneficial arrangements. Take time to understand their business goals and challenges - perhaps they're struggling to fill certain time slots, looking for additional revenue streams, or wanting to attract new demographics to their facility.

When you understand what venue owners need, you can position your aerial arts classes as solutions rather than simply requesting space rental. Maintain professional, respectful communication throughout all interactions, and be completely transparent about your business model and growth plans. Venue owners appreciate honesty about your student numbers, revenue projections, and long-term vision because it helps them assess the partnership's potential value.

Pricing Negotiations

Start your pricing discussions with hourly rates, which provide flexibility for both parties during the initial stages of your relationship. As your classes grow and prove successful, you can move toward block bookings that offer better rates in exchange for commitment.

Marketing partnerships and cross-promotion opportunities often provide more value than simple rent reductions. Offering to promote the venue to your students, include their branding in your materials, or provide reciprocal marketing can create win-win situations that strengthen the partnership. However, be prepared to walk away if the terms don't support your business model - desperation leads to poor agreements that can harm your long-term success. Consider long-term partnerships only after you've proven your ability to deliver consistent attendance and revenue.

Chapter 3

VENUE MASTERY

Negotiation Strategies That Work

Contract Considerations

Keep your initial agreements simple and flexible, avoiding complex terms that might create problems later. Include clear cancellation terms that protect both parties while providing reasonable notice periods. Specify equipment storage and setup arrangements in detail, including who's responsible for moving equipment, where it can be stored between classes, and any restrictions on installation methods.

Address insurance and liability clearly, ensuring both parties understand their responsibilities and coverage requirements.

Learn from my experience with Dance Inspires - ensure maintenance responsibilities are explicitly defined, including who handles repairs, cleaning, and facility upkeep. Ambiguity in these areas can lead to disputes that damage otherwise good partnerships.

Access your free subscripton to Aerial Studio Boost online for free resources

Chapter 3
VENUE MASTERY

Multi-Venue Management

As you scale to multiple venues, management becomes more complex:

Scheduling Coordination
- Use centralised booking system (Go Team Up)
- Coordinate instructor schedules across venues
- Manage equipment transport and storage
- Plan for travel time between locations

Quality Control
- Maintain consistent standards across all venues
- Regular venue audits and assessments
- Standardised setup and safety procedures
- Student feedback monitoring

Relationship Management
- Regular check-ins with venue owners
- Address issues promptly and professionally
- Maintain good relationships for long-term success
- Be prepared to make changes when necessary

Chapter 3

VENUE MASTERY

Red Flags to Avoid (Lessons from Dance Inspires)

Venue Red Flags
- Structural concerns or damage
- Poor maintenance or cleanliness
- Unreliable or unprofessional management
- History of building problems or dispute

Business Red Flags
- Inflexible pricing or terms
- Poor communication or responsiveness
- Unrealistic restrictions or requirements
- History of disputes with other renters
- Absent or unresponsive landlords

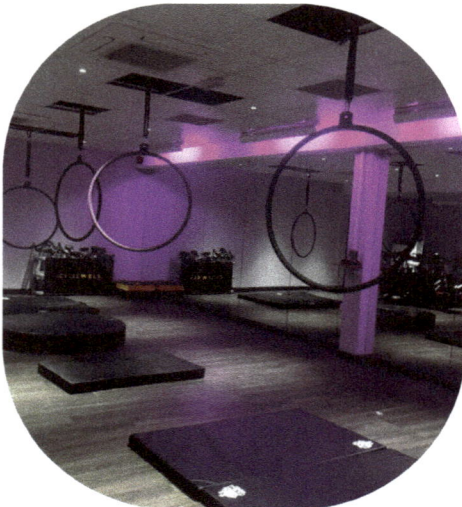

Location Red Flags
- Poor parking or accessibility
- Unsafe neighbourhood or lighting
- Noise restrictions that limit class times
- Competing businesses in the immediate area

Equipment Considerations for Rental Venues

Portable Equipment Setup
- Portable Poles: X-Pole or R-Poles / Firetoys for aerial
- Aerial Points: Portable rigging systems where possible
- Safety Equipment: Crash mats and first aid supplies
- Sound System: Portable speakers with wireless connectivity

Storage Solutions
- Negotiate storage space at venues
- Invest in equipment transport systems
- Consider equipment sharing between venues
- Plan for setup and breakdown time

Installation Requirements
- Minimise permanent installations
- Use certified rigging professionals
- Maintain installation documentation
- Regular safety inspections

Chapter 3
VENUE MASTERY

Building Long-Term Partnerships
Proving Your Value

The foundation of successful venue partnerships rests on consistently demonstrating your value through professional service delivery. Show up on time, maintain high instruction standards, and ensure classes run smoothly without creating extra work for venue staff. Positive student feedback reflects well on the venue, while reliable payment and clear communication establish the trust needed for future negotiations. Your contribution to their overall success - bringing new customers, filling unused time slots, creating a positive atmosphere - becomes leverage for stronger partnerships.

Expanding Relationships

As demand grows, naturally expand by increasing class frequency and adding workshops or special events. These higher-value bookings boost revenue for both parties while demonstrating market demand. Provide marketing support by promoting the venue to your students and including their branding in materials. Consider exclusive partnerships for prime venues where relationships have proven particularly successful, providing you with preferred scheduling while giving venues confidence in your commitment.

Transition Planning

Build towards longer-term agreements once you've established a track record of success. Proven ability to maintain consistent attendance gives you negotiating power for better rates and terms. Revenue-sharing arrangements often become attractive at this stage, aligning both parties' interests in growth. Plan for eventual dedicated space only after proving sustainable success across multiple venues - the partnership experience provides invaluable knowledge for any
future facility decisions.

Chapter 3

VENUE MASTERY

The Foundation for Growth

Your venue strategy isn't just about finding a place to teach - it's about creating the foundation for sustainable growth. The hourly rental model gives you the flexibility to test, learn, and scale without the financial pressure of long-term commitments.

My experience with Dance Inspires taught me that the wrong venue can drain your resources and energy. But the right venue partnerships - like those with Oxford Academy, Leys Leisure Centre and Feel Fit Gym - can become the foundation for building something extraordinary.

Every venue relationship you build becomes part of your network. Every successful class you run proves your concept. Every student you serve becomes an advocate for your business.

Remember: The perfect venue doesn't exist, but the right venue for your current stage of business does. Start where you can, prove your concept, and scale strategically. And whatever you do, learn from my mistakes - avoid long-term leases until you've proven your model works.

In the next chapter, we'll dive into safety protocols - the non-negotiable systems that protect your students, your instructors, and your business. Because no venue or cheap bit of kit is worth compromising safety.

Access your free subscripton to Aerial Studio Boost online for free resources

Your Venue Action Plan

Week 1: Research and Mapping
- ☐ Identify 3-4 potential venues in your area
- ☐ Research ceiling heights and basic facilities
- ☐ Create a contact list with phone numbers and emails
- ☐ Map venues by location and target demographics

Week 2: Initial Outreach
- ☐ Contact venues to explain your concept
- ☐ Request viewing appointments
- ☐ Prepare insurance certificates and business information
- ☐ Schedule venue visits

Week 3: Venue Evaluations
- ☐ Visit and evaluate each potential venue
- ☐ Measure ceiling heights and assess facilities
- ☐ Discuss pricing and availability
- ☐ Take photos and notes for comparison

Week 4: Negotiations and Trials
- ☐ Negotiate trial arrangements with the top 3 venues
- ☐ Finalise initial agreements
- ☐ Plan equipment setup and logistics
- ☐ Schedule first classes

Safety First - The Non-Negotiables

In aerial arts, safety isn't just important - it's everything. One accident can destroy years of reputation-building and put students at serious risk. Here's how to create bulletproof safety systems that protect everyone.

Why Safety is Your Business Foundation

Imagine this scenario: A new student joins your intermediate class despite being a beginner. They attempt an inversion without proper preparation, fall, and sustain a serious injury. Without proper safety protocols, you could face liability claims, insurance issues, and devastating damage to your reputation.

This is exactly why safety systems aren't optional - they're the foundation of everything we do.

Today, with 1000+ students across multiple venues, we've built comprehensive safety systems that protect everyone. That's not luck - it's systematic preparation.

Chapter 4
SAFETY FIRST - THE NON-NEGOTIABLES

The Three Pillars of Aerial Safety

→ **Equipment Safety**

Rigging Standards:

- Only certified rigging professionals install aerial points
- Annual inspections by qualified engineers
- Load ratings clearly documented and never exceeded
- Backup systems for all primary rigging points

Equipment Maintenance:

- Daily visual inspections before each class
- Monthly detailed equipment checks
- Immediate replacement of worn or damaged items
- Detailed maintenance logs for insurance purposes

→ **Instructor Safety Training**

Our 10-Week Training Program Includes:

- Risk assessment and hazard identification
- Spotting techniques and emergency procedures
- Student assessment / progression protocols
- Injury prevention and first aid basics
- Documentation and incident reporting

Ongoing Requirements:

- First aid certification (renewed every 3 years)
- Regular safety refresher training
- DBS checks for youth instructors
- Clear protocols for handling incidents

Chapter 4

SAFETY FIRST - THE NON-NEGOTIABLES

The Three Pillars of Aerial Safety

→ **Student Safety Protocols**

Pre-Class Requirements:

- Comprehensive waiver and health screening
- Safety briefing for all new students
- Jewellery and loose clothing removal
- Proper footwear (or barefoot) enforcement

During Class:

- Maximum 15 students per instructor
- Progressive skill building - no shortcuts
- Constant supervision during inversions
- Clear "stop" signals and respect for limits

Chapter 4

SAFETY FIRST - THE NON-NEGOTIABLES

Waivers and Health Screening: Your First Line of Defense

Digital-First Approach

Our primary system operates through Go Team Up, where students cannot book their first class until completing a comprehensive digital screening process. This includes a detailed liability waiver, health and safety questionnaire, emergency contact information, and medical condition disclosure that helps instructors provide appropriate modifications.

Paper Backup System

For students preferring traditional paperwork or experiencing technical difficulties, printed waivers are available at all venues. These contain the same comprehensive screening and liability protections, must be completed before the first class, and are scanned and stored digitally for consistent record-keeping.

Comprehensive Health Coverage

Our screening covers previous injuries or medical conditions requiring modifications, current medications affecting balance or coordination, pregnancy status requiring specific protocols, fitness level and exercise experience to gauge appropriate starting points, and complete emergency contact details for incident response.

Chapter 4

SAFETY FIRST - THE NON-NEGOTIABLES

Essential Safety Equipment

→ **For Every Class:**

- Crash mats under all aerial points
- First aid kit easily accessible
- Emergency contact information
- Incident report forms
- Phone for emergency calls

→ **Venue-Specific:**

- Proper lighting (no dark shadows under rigging points)
- Clear floor space around all equipment
- Temperature control (overheating/under-heating increases injury risk)
- Easy access to exits

Chapter 4

SAFETY FIRST - THE NON-NEGOTIABLES

Risk Management Systems

→ **Student Assessment**

- Fitness and flexibility screening through health forms
- Previous injury disclosure via Go Team Up system
- Skill level evaluation during the first class
- Regular progress reviews

→ **Class Structure Safety**

- Standardised warm-up (minimum 10 minutes)
- Progressive skill introduction
- Mandatory cool-down and stretching
- Clear class level definitions

→ **Emergency Procedures**

- Written emergency action plans
- Staff trained in basic first aid
- Clear communication with venue management
- Direct contact with local emergency services

Chapter 4
SAFETY FIRST - THE NON-NEGOTIABLES

Go Team Up Integration for Safety

Automated Safety Compliance

Go Team Up ensures complete safety compliance by preventing students from booking any classes until they've completed all required waivers and health screenings. The system automatically flags important health information, making medical conditions and safety considerations immediately visible to instructors in the booking interface. Emergency contacts are stored within each student's profile and medical conditions are prominently highlighted throughout the booking system, ensuring critical information is never overlooked.

Instructor Dashboard

The instructor dashboard provides quick access to essential student health information, displaying injury history and physical limitations clearly before each class begins. Emergency contact details are readily available with just a few clicks, while the integrated incident reporting system allows instructors to document any issues immediately within the same platform. This seamless integration ensures safety information flows efficiently from initial booking through class delivery and any necessary follow-up procedures.

Chapter 4

SAFETY FIRST - THE NON-NEGOTIABLES

Insurance and Legal Protection

→ ### Essential Coverage:

- Public liability (minimum £5 million)
- Professional indemnity
- Equipment insurance
- Employer's liability (for staff)

→ ### Documentation Requirements:

- Signed waivers for all students (digital or paper)
- Incident reports for any injuries
- Equipment inspection records
- Staff training certificates

Chapter 4

SAFETY FIRST - THE NON-NEGOTIABLES

Your Safety Checklist Action Plan

Before Opening:
☐ Professional rigging inspection completed
☐ All instructors first aid certified /
certifications stored
☐ Comprehensive waivers prepared
(digital and paper)
☐ Go Team Up safety integration configured
☐ Emergency procedures documented
☐ Insurance policies active

Daily Operations:
☐ Equipment visual inspection
☐ Safety briefing for new students
☐ Incident report forms available
☐ Emergency contacts accessible
☐ Clear communication of class limits

Monthly Reviews:
☐ Equipment detailed inspection
☐ Staff safety training updates
☐ Incident pattern analysis
☐ Insurance policy review
☐ Emergency procedure practice

Chapter 4

The Bottom Line

Safety isn't about fear - it's about creating an environment where students can push their boundaries with confidence. When students trust your safety systems, they're more likely to stay, refer friends, and invest in their aerial journey.

Remember: It's better to be overly cautious than to deal with a preventable injury. Your reputation, your business, and most importantly, your students' wellbeing depend on getting this right.

"In the next chapter, we'll explore how to build and manage your instructor team - the people who bring your safety systems to life and create the magic that keeps students coming back."

~ Nicola Ghalmi

Access your free subscripton to Aerial Studio Boost online for free resources

PART 2: OPERATIONS (Chapters 5-8)

→

Chapter 5

Chapter 5: Building Your Dream Team

Your instructors are the heart of your business. They're the ones who create the magic, build relationships with students, and ultimately determine whether your academy thrives or fails. Here's how to find, train, and retain exceptional aerial arts instructors.

Why Your Team Makes or Breaks Your Business

When I started Aerial Arts Academy, I thought the hardest part would be finding venues or managing finances. I was wrong. The biggest challenge - and the biggest opportunity - is building a team of instructors who share your vision and deliver exceptional experiences.

Today, our team of 23+ instructors across multiple venues maintains consistent quality while each brings their unique personality to classes. That doesn't happen by accident - it happens through intentional recruitment, comprehensive training, and most importantly, exceptional retention strategies.

Access your free subscripton to Aerial Studio Boost online for free resources

Chapter 5: Building Your Dream Team

Finding Your First Star: The Kat Kelly Story

My lead instructor Kat, came to me through a simple coffee meeting (although looking back I do think it was divine intervention / the Universe answering my wishes). We met at Costa for what was supposed to be an informal chat about teaching aerial arts. By the time I left that coffee shop, I had one thought:
"I must have her on my team."

That instinct was right. Kat has been invaluable ever since, and her testimonial captures exactly what great team building looks like:

"I have watched Nicola grow an incredible team from scratch and her leadership skills are admirable. She is approachable and considerate and has time for everyone's ideas and concerns. Yet she still manages to maintain a professional relationship and clear boundaries with the team to uphold high standards and work ethics. She is a power house of energy and ideas and her ability to juggle multiple things without sacrificing attention to any of them is a strength of hers."

Kat Kelly, Lead Instructor, Aerial Arts Academy

The tip: find a team of Kats who share your passion and vision.

Chapter 5

OPERATIONS

The Instructor Profile That Works

→ **Technical Skills (Non-Negotiable):**

- Relevant aerial arts qualifications
- Minimum 2 years personal practice experience
- Ability to demonstrate all moves they teach
- Understanding of anatomy and injury prevention

→ **Teaching Abilities:**

- Clear communication skills
- Patience
- Ability to modify moves for different abilities
- Natural enthusiasm for aerial arts

→ **Personal Qualities:**

- Reliability and professionalism
- Positive, encouraging attitude
- Safety-first mindset
- Commitment to ongoing learning

Access your free subscripton to Aerial Studio Boost online for free resources

Chapter 5

OPERATIONS

The Instructor Profile That Works

Our 10-Week Training Program

Every entry-level instructor has the opportunity to complete the Aerial Arts Academy comprehensive training program before teaching independently:

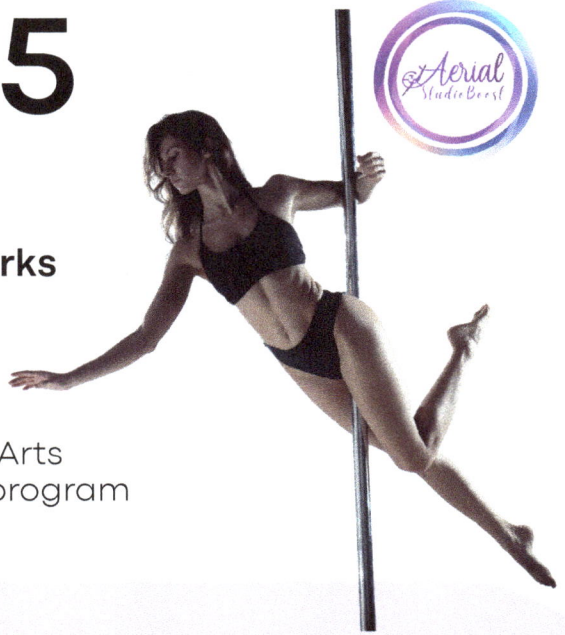

"I completed the Trainee Pole Instructor Programme at Aerial Arts Academy and would highly recommend it to anyone interested in becoming a pole instructor at AAA. The programme provided clear guidance, comprehensive learning materials, and continuous support throughout the training (and even beyond). It offered invaluable hands-on experience and practical knowledge that no official certificate alone could provide. This programme truly prepares you for the realities of teaching pole in a supportive and professional environment."

Belen Esteve, Aerial Arts Academy Instructor

Our comprehensive training program covers:

- Aerial Arts Academy teaching philosophy and standards
- Complete syllabus training across all disciplines and levels
- Shadowing experienced instructors in live classes
- Risk assessment, hazard identification, and emergency procedures
- Student health screening interpretation and safety protocols
- Class structure, progression planning, and curriculum delivery
- Spotting techniques, physical assistance, and hands-on support
- Verbal cueing, demonstration skills, and effective communication
- Managing mixed-ability classes and individual student needs

Chapter 5

OPERATIONS

Our comprehensive training program coverage continues:

- Assessing student readiness for progression and new movements
- Modification techniques for injuries, limitations, and adaptations
- Building confidence in nervous students and managing challenging personalities
- Customer service excellence and professional communication
- Handling complaints, concerns, and difficult situations
- Promoting additional services including private lessons and workshops
- Go Team Up system operation and administrative procedures
- Supervised teaching practice with feedback and assessment
- Ongoing support, mentorship, and professional development

Chapter 5

OPERATIONS

Self-Employed Structure: Why It Works

All our instructors work as self-employed contractors, which benefits everyone:

→ **For the Business:**

- Reduced employment obligations and paperwork
- Flexibility in scheduling and coverage
- Performance-based relationship
- Lower administrative burden

→ **For Instructors:**

- Flexibility to work with multiple studios
- Control over their schedule and availability
- Ability to build their own brand
- Tax advantages of self-employment

→ **Legal Requirements:**

- Clear contracts defining the relationship
- Payment per class taught (£15-45/hour depending on experience)
- Freedom to accept or decline work

Chapter 5

OPERATIONS

Staff Retention: As Important as Student Retention

Here's what most studio owners get wrong: they focus obsessively on student retention while treating instructors as replaceable.
This is backwards thinking.

Your instructors allow you to work ON your business, not IN it - which is fundamental to success. When you have a stable, happy team, you can focus on growth, strategy, and expansion instead of constantly recruiting and training new people.

My Staff Retention Philosophy: Facilitate Their Needs

My job isn't to manage my instructors - it's to facilitate their needs. When I take care of them, they take care of our students. Here's my a win-win system that creates sustainable growth:

→ **Mental /Financial Support:**

- Financial support towards certifications
- Mental health support / understanding
- Career development planning
- Recognition and appreciation

→ **Professional Development:**

- Teacher-only training sessions
- Skill-building workshops
- Skills workshop attendance support
- Peer learning opportunities
- Unlimited class allowance

→ **Work Environment:**

- Appropriate pay rates (based on experience)
- Scheduling flexibility around their other commitments
- Open environment that encourages feedback and ideas
- Clear communication channels

→ **Empowerment:**

- Autonomy in their teaching approach (within safety guidelines)
- Input on class development and programming
- Leadership opportunities as the team grows
- Respect for their expertise and experience

Chapter 5

OPERATIONS

Creating an Open Feedback Culture

I actively encourage feedback and ideas from my team.
Some of our best innovations have come from instructor suggestions:

- New class formats and progressions
- Student engagement strategies
- Safety improvements
- Operational efficiencies

When instructors feel heard and valued, they become invested in the business's success, not just their individual classes.

The Business Impact of Great Retention

→   **Consistency for Students:**

- Familiar faces build trust and community
- Consistent teaching quality across all classes
- Reduced disruption from instructor changes
- Stronger student-instructor relationships

→   **Operational Efficiency:**

- Less time spent on recruitment and training
- Reduced administrative burden
- Better class coverage and scheduling
- Improved team communication

"Your staff are just as important as students... if not more important! Without them, your business does not thrive!"
~ Nicola Ghalmi

→   **Business Growth:**

- Instructors become brand ambassadors
- Word-of-mouth referrals from happy team members
- Ability to focus on expansion rather than replacement
- Stronger reputation in the aerial arts community

Chapter 5

OPERATIONS

Managing Multiple Venues

→ **Consistency Across Locations:**

- Standardised training for all instructors
- Regular cross-venue teaching opportunities
- Shared resources and teaching materials
- Unified brand presentation

→ **Communication Systems:**

- WhatsApp group chat
- Aerial Education Hub for chats / standard operating systems
- Team meetings
- Clear escalation procedures for issues

When Things Don't Work Out

Despite best efforts, sometimes instructor relationships don't work:

→ **Common Issues:**

- Inconsistent availability or reliability
- Safety concerns or protocol violations
- Poor student feedback despite support
- Personality conflicts that can't be resolved

→ **Professional Separation:**

- Document all issues and support provided
- Have honest conversations about expectations
- Provide clear timelines for improvement
- End relationships professionally when necessary

Access your free subscripton to Aerial Studio Boost online for free resources

Your Team Building Action Plan

Month 1: Foundation
☐ Define your ideal instructor profile
☐ Create job descriptions and contracts
☐ Develop an interview and assessment process
☐ Set up training program structure

Month 2: Recruitment
☐ Network within aerial arts communities
☐ Screen applications and conduct interviews
☐ Select initial team members
☐ Begin your comprehensive training program

Month 3: Retention Systems
☐ Implement feedback and support systems
☐ Establish team communication channels
☐ Plan ongoing development activities
☐ Create recognition and reward programs

Chapter 5

OPERATIONS

The Long-Term Vision

Your instructor team isn't just about covering classes - they're your business partners in creating transformational experiences for students. When you invest in them, support their growth, and create an environment where they can thrive, they become your greatest asset.

The best instructors will become advocates for your business, help you expand to new venues as you scale. They're the ones who make it possible for you to step back from day-to-day operations and focus on strategic growth.

Remember: Facilitate their needs, and they'll deliver for your students. It's the foundation of sustainable success.

Conclusion

In the next chapter, we'll explore how to create class structures and curricula that keep students engaged, progressing, and coming back for more.

Chapter 6

OPERATIONS

Chapter 6: Creating Your Class Structure and Curriculum

A great class isn't just about teaching moves - it's about creating an experience that builds confidence, community, and keeps students coming back. Here's how to design classes that work for beginners and advanced students alike.

The Foundation of Great Classes

After teaching thousands of classes across multiple venues, I've learned that successful aerial arts classes follow a proven structure. It's not about being the most advanced instructor - it's about creating consistent, safe, and engaging experiences that help students progress.

Access your free subscripton to Aerial Studio Boost online for free resources

Chapter 6

OPERATIONS

The 60-Minute Class Formula

→ **Minutes 1-10: Warm-Up (Non-Negotiable)**

- Joint mobility, pulse raiser and dynamic stretching
- Aerial-specific conditioning
- Mental preparation and focus
- Safety reminders and equipment checks

→ **Minutes 11-45: Main Content**

- Skill introduction and demonstration
- Progressive practice with spotting
- Individual modifications and assistance
- Strength and flexibility integration

→ **Minutes 46-60: Cool-Down and Integration**

- Gentle stretching and recovery
- Skill review and celebration
- Next class preview
- Community building time

Chapter 6

OPERATIONS

Progressive Level Structure

BEGINNER CLASSES (LEVELS 1-4)	INTERMEDIATE CLASSES (LEVELS 5-8)	ADVANCED CLASSES (LEVEL 9 +)
FOCUS: SAFETY, BASIC STRENGTH, FUNDAMENTAL MOVES	**FOCUS:** FLOW DEVELOPMENT, STRENGTH BUILDING, COMBINATION MOVES	**FOCUS:** COMPLEX MOVES, PERFORMANCE SKILLS, PERSONAL STYLE
CLASS SIZE: MAXIMUM 15 STUDENTS	**CLASS SIZE:** MAXIMUM 15 STUDENTS	**CLASS SIZE:** MAXIMUM 15 STUDENTS
EQUIPMENT: LOWER AERIAL POINTS, EXTRA MATS	**EQUIPMENT:** STANDARD HEIGHT, VARIED APPARATUS	**EQUIPMENT:** FULL HEIGHT, SPECIALISED APPARATUS
KEY ELEMENTS: - EXTENSIVE SAFETY BRIEFINGS - BASIC GRIP AND BODY POSITIONING - SIMPLE SEQUENCES AND HOLDS - CONFIDENCE BUILDING EXERCISES	**KEY ELEMENTS:** - DYNAMIC SEQUENCES - STRENGTH CHALLENGES - CREATIVE FLOW DEVELOPMENT - PEER LEARNING OPPORTUNITIES	**KEY ELEMENTS:** - ADVANCED TECHNIQUE REFINEMENT - PERFORMANCE PREPARATION - CREATIVE CHOREOGRAPHY - MENTORSHIP OPPORTUNITIES

Chapter 6

OPERATIONS

Curriculum Development by Discipline

→ ### Pole Dance and Fitness
Beginner Progression: Weeks 1-6:

- Basic spins and holds (Fireman spin, pole seat)
- Floor work and transitions (Dip & Flick / leg circles / floor cartwheels)
- Simple holds and poses (Lift & Slide / Model pose)
- Combination sequences

→ ### Aerial Hoop (Lyra)
Beginner Progression: Weeks 1-6:**

- Basic holds and positions such as Delilah / Delilah Climb / Star On The Bar / Gazelle / Seats in Hoop, climbs, poses.
- Focusing on building basic strength climbs.
- Basic sequence building

Intermediate/Advanced Progression:

- Dynamic entries and exits
- Complex transitions
- Strength-based holds
- Flow development

Chapter 6

OPERATIONS

→ **Aerial Silks**
Beginner Progression: Weeks 1-6:

- Fabric familiarisation and basic climbs (working in the hitch / russian and french climbs)
- Simple wraps and holds (Rebecca Gazelle for example)
- Basic drops (low level Goddess bomb drop release)
- equence building

Safety Considerations:

- Higher instructor-to-student ratios
- Extensive drop training
- Progressive height introduction
- Mandatory safety assessments

Youth Program Structure (Ages 8-15)

- Class Format: 60 minutes with games and additional breaks
- Class Size: Maximum 10 students
- Focus Areas: Fitness, confidence building, social skills, goal achievement

Key Modifications:

- Increased break time and game integration
- Age-appropriate music and themes
- Enhanced safety protocols and supervision
- Parent communication systems

↰ ***FREE LESSON
PLANS HERE***

Chapter 6

OPERATIONS

Class Management Strategies

→ **Mixed-Level Classes**

Challenge: Different skill levels in one class

Solutions:

- Offer variations for every move
- Use advanced students as peer mentors
- Create optional challenges
- Provide individual attention

→ **Injury Management**

Prevention:

- Proper warm-up protocols
- Progressive skill building
- Regular fitness assessments
- Clear communication about limitations

Chapter 6

OPERATIONS

The Aerial Education Hub Integration

Our online platform enhances in-person classes by providing:
- Pre-class preparation videos
- Post-class practice sequences
- Flexibility and strength training
- Progress tracking tools

Developed during Covid, this platform gave a way to provide monthly members a thank you for sticking by us - we didnt lose a single member during Covid!! Providing your members with additional benefits and resources allows you to create a value add that is priceless and keeps them coming back (forever!)

Creating Community Through Classes

BEFORE CLASS:	DURING CLASS:	AFTER CLASS:
• WELCOME NEW STUDENTS PERSONALLY • ENCOURAGE PEER INTRODUCTIONS • CREATE INCLUSIVE ENVIRONMENT • SET POSITIVE EXPECTATIONS	• CELEBRATE INDIVIDUAL ACHIEVEMENTS • ENCOURAGE PEER SUPPORT • MAINTAIN POSITIVE ENERGY • ADDRESS CHALLENGES CONSTRUCTIVELY	• PROVIDE SPECIFIC FEEDBACK • SUGGEST NEXT STEPS • ENCOURAGE SOCIAL CONNECTION • GATHER FEEDBACK FOR IMPROVEMENT

Chapter 6

OPERATIONS

Seasonal Programming

QUARTERLY WORKSHOPS:*	ANNUAL EVENTS:
• VALENTINE'S PARTNER CLASSES	• ANNUAL EVENTS AND SHOWCASE
• SUMMER STRENGTH INTENSIVES	• STUDENT APPRECIATION EVENTS
• HALLOWEEN THEMED SESSIONS	• INSTRUCTOR TRAINING INTENSIVES
• CHRISTMAS PERFORMANCE PREPARATION	• COMMUNITY OUTREACH PROGRAMS

Quality Control Systems

Maintaining consistent quality across all classes and venues requires systematic approaches to instructor standards and student experience.

Our team implement standardised class plans that ensure every student receives the same high-quality experience regardless of which instructor they have or which venue they attend. This includes regular observation and feedback sessions where I, or my lead instructor, personally assess classes and provide constructive guidance to instructors. Student feedback is actively integrated into our improvement process through post-class surveys and regular check-ins, allowing us to identify areas for enhancement and celebrate successes. The entire system operates on continuous improvement protocols, meaning we're constantly refining our approach based on real-world results and student outcomes.

Student Progress Tracking:
- Level assessment criteria
- Progress documentation
- Achievement recognition (we offer certificates upon level completion)
- Advancement celebrations

Your Curriculum Development Action Plan

Week 1-2: Foundation Planning

- ☐ Define level progressions for each discipline
- ☐ Create standardised class structures
- ☐ Develop safety protocols
- ☐ Plan assessment criteria

Week 3-4: Content Creation

- ☐ Write detailed class plans
- ☐ Create modification options
- ☐ Develop warm-up and cool-down routines
- ☐ Plan progression sequences

Week 5-6: Testing and Refinement

- ☐ Pilot classes with feedback collection
- ☐ Refine based on student responses
- ☐ Train instructors on new curriculum
- ☐ Implement quality control systems

Chapter 6

OPERATIONS

The Long-Term Vision

Your curriculum isn't just about teaching moves - it's about creating transformational experiences that build confidence, community, and lifelong passion for aerial arts. When students feel supported, challenged, and celebrated, they become your best advocates.

Great curriculum creates:

- Consistent student progression
- Instructor confidence and success
- Strong community bonds
- Sustainable business growth

Remember: every class is an opportunity to change someone's life. Make it count.

Conclusion:

In the next chapter, we'll explore pricing strategies that attract students while ensuring your business remains profitable and sustainable.

Chapter 7

PRICING STRATEGIES THAT WORK

The Psychology of Pricing

Pricing isn't just about covering costs - it's about positioning your business and creating perceived value. After years of testing different models across multiple venues, I've learned that transparent, fair pricing builds trust and loyalty better than complex discount structures.

Membership Structure That Converts

Your pricing should reflect commitment levels while remaining accessible. My current structure works because it rewards regular attendance without penalising occasional students. The updated membership tiers are: 1 class per week at £40 monthly, 2 classes at £65, 3 classes at £80, 4 classes at £85, 5 classes at £110, 6 classes at £130, and unlimited access at £154 monthly.

These tiers create natural progression points where students see clear value in upgrading. The sweet spot is typically the 2-3 class memberships, where students feel committed but not overwhelmed. Notice how the jump from 4 to 5 classes is significant - this encourages students to either stay at 4 or commit to unlimited.

Access your free subscripton to Aerial Studio Boost online for free resources

Chapter 7

PRICING STRATEGIES THAT WORK

Pay-As-You-Go Strategy

Not everyone wants a membership, and that's fine. PAYG at £15 per class serves multiple purposes: it's accessible for newcomers, provides flexibility for irregular attendees, and creates a clear value proposition for memberships. When students realise they're paying £60 monthly for 4 PAYG classes versus £40 for a 4-class a month membership with additional benefits, the choice becomes obvious.

Youth and Adult Pricing Parity

Youth classes are priced the same as adult classes. This reflects the equal quality of instruction, venue costs, and class duration. While some studios discount youth pricing, I've found that parents appreciate consistent pricing and don't expect discounts when they see the professional setup and qualified instructors. Sibling discounts are however, a great way to go!

Private Lesson Premium

Private lessons at £35 for members and £45 for non-members create a premium revenue stream while serving students who need personalised attention. The member discount reinforces membership value while the non-member rate reflects the true cost of one-on-one instruction.

Chapter 7

PRICING STRATEGIES THAT WORK

Free Trial Strategy

Our free first class using code OAA1STFREE removes the barrier to entry completely. This strategy works because aerial arts is experiential - people need to feel the equipment and experience the instruction quality to understand the value. The conversion rate from free trial to paid membership is consistently high because the experience sells itself. Go Team Up is fantastic for generation of coupon codes and has been fundamental in our lead generation strategy.

Seasonal Adjustments and Promotions

Rather than constant discounting, I focus on value-added promotions. Free workshops for members, extended trial periods during slow seasons, and referral bonuses maintain pricing integrity while driving enrollment. Discounting your core pricing devalues your service and attracts price-sensitive customers who leave when cheaper options appear.

Revenue Optimisation

The key to sustainable pricing is understanding your cost structure and desired profit margins, then building pricing that supports both. Track your average revenue per student, lifetime customer value, and membership retention rates. These metrics tell you whether your pricing strategy is working long-term, not just driving short-term sales.

Your pricing communicates your brand positioning. Price too low, and people question quality. Price too high without demonstrable value, and you limit accessibility. The goal is finding the sweet spot where students feel they're receiving excellent value while you maintain healthy margins for growth and reinvestment.

Chapter 8

SYSTEMS & TECHNOLOGY

"The right systems don't just make your business run smoother - they free you to focus on growth instead of administration. Here's how to build a technology stack that scales with your success."

Why Systems Matter More Than You Think

During my time as owner of Dance Inspires, I managed everything manually - student bookings on paper, payments in cash, communication through personal messages. After a few months of drowning in administration, I moved to BookWhen, which helped but still had limitations. When I launched Aerial Arts Academy, I chose Go Team Up from the start because of its superior functionality and integration capabilities.

Today, with over 1000+ students across multiple venues, our automated systems handle the majority of routine tasks while providing insights that drive strategic decisions. The technology investment pays for itself through time savings and improved customer experience.

Chapter 8
SYSTEMS & TECHNOLOGY

Go Team Up: Your Business Command Center

After experiencing the limitations of manual systems and BookWhen, Go Team Up became our foundation because it handles everything from class scheduling to payment processing in one integrated system. The platform manages our entire customer journey from first inquiry to long-term membership renewal.

The system handles our complex scheduling across multiple venues with different instructors, equipment requirements, and capacity limits. Students can book classes, join waitlists, and receive automatic notifications about schedule changes. The mobile app ensures students can manage their bookings anywhere, reducing no-shows and last-minute cancellations.

Go Team Up seamlessly manages our tiered membership structure from £40 monthly single classes to £154 unlimited access. The system automatically tracks usage, sends renewal reminders, and handles membership upgrades or downgrades without manual intervention.

Customer Management and Communication

New students receive automated welcome sequences that introduce them to our community, explain safety protocols, and encourage their second class booking. This automation ensures consistent communication while I focus on teaching and business development.

The system allows targeted messaging based on student behavior, membership level, and class preferences. Members receive different communications than pay-as-you-go students, and inactive students get re-engagement campaigns automatically.

Our mandatory waivers and health screening forms are built into the registration process. Students cannot book their first class until these are completed, ensuring legal compliance while streamlining the check-in process.

Chapter 8

SYSTEMS & TECHNOLOGY

Payment Processing and Automation

Go Team Up integrates with GoCardless, PayPal and Stripe for secure payment processing, handling everything from single-class payments to recurring membership charges. The system automatically retries failed payments and sends emails for expired cards.

The system handles monthly membership renewals, class credits, refunds, and membership freezes according to your policies, maintaining detailed records for accounting purposes.

Data Tracking and Analytics

Go Team Up provides essential metrics including class attendance rates, membership retention, revenue per student, and instructor performance. These insights drive decisions about class scheduling, pricing adjustments, and marketing focus.

The platform tracks booking patterns, no-show rates, and class preferences, allowing you to optimise schedules and identify opportunities for new offerings. Understanding when students typically book helps with capacity planning and marketing timing. The system identifies at-risk students through booking pattern analysis, enabling proactive retention efforts.

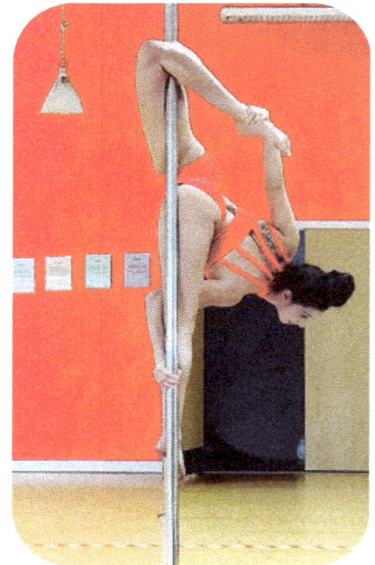

Integration with Other Systems

Go Team Up integrates with Brevo for advanced email marketing campaigns. Student data flows automatically between systems using Zapier, enabling sophisticated segmentation and personalised communication without manual data entry. We have even used Zapier to link Go Team Up with the Aerial Education Hub so membership purchasers get a welcome email and access to that too!

Chapter 8

SYSTEMS & TECHNOLOGY

Scaling Considerations

As you expand to multiple locations, Go Team Up handles complex scheduling across venues with different instructors, venues, and capacity requirements. The system maintains consistency while allowing location-specific customisation.

Real-time booking data helps identify peak demand periods and optimise class schedules. The waitlist functionality captures demand that exceeds capacity, informing decisions about additional classes or venue expansion.

Learning from System Transitions

Having experienced manual systems, BookWhen, and Go Team Up, I can confidently say that investing in the right platform from the beginning saves significant time and money. Each system transition required data migration, staff retraining, and customer communication, which could have been avoided with better initial planning.

The key lesson is choosing systems that can grow with your business rather than requiring replacement as you scale. Go Team Up's comprehensive functionality and integration capabilities have supported our growth from startup to over 1000+ students without requiring platform changes. I'm sure there are plenty of systems out there that do similar to GTU - the trick is to test out the capabilities to see if they fit your needs.

Chapter 8

SYSTEMS & TECHNOLOGY

Your Systems Implementation Action Plan

Week 1-2: Foundation Setup

☐ Sign up for Go Team Up account and complete basic setup

☐ Configure class categories, pricing tiers, and venue information

☐ Set up instructor profiles and availability schedules

☐ Create basic policies for cancellations, refunds, and membership terms

☐ Test payment processing integration

☐ Design and implement mandatory waiver and health screening forms

Week 3-4: Advanced Configuration

☐ Set up membership tiers and automated billing cycles

☐ Configure email automation sequences for new students

☐ Create waitlist management and notification systems

☐ Integrate with Brevo for advanced email marketing

☐ Set up reporting dashboards and key performance indicators

☐ Configure mobile app settings and push notifications

Your Systems Implementation Action Plan

Week 5-6: Integration and Testing
☐ Connect Go Team Up with accounting software (Xero for example)
☐ Create Zapier workflows for advanced automation
☐ Test all booking flows from student perspective
☐ Train staff on system usage and troubleshooting
☐ Conduct soft launch with existing students for feedback

Week 7-8: Launch and Optimisation
☐ Launch full marketing campaigns driving new registrations
☐ Monitor system performance and user experience
☐ Analyse initial data and optimise class schedules
☐ Refine automated communication sequences based on response rates
☐ Set up regular reporting and review processes
☐ Document procedures for ongoing system maintenance

Month 2: Performance Review and Scaling
☐ Review key metrics and identify optimisation opportunities
☐ Expand automation workflows based on usage patterns

Chapter 8

SYSTEMS & TECHNOLOGY

Your Systems Implementation Action Plan

☐ Implement advanced features like loyalty programs
☐ Plan for multi-venue expansion if applicable
☐ Conduct staff training on advanced system features
☐ Prepare for seasonal adjustments and promotional campaigns

Your systems should work for you, not against you. When technology handles routine tasks efficiently, you can focus on what matters most: creating exceptional experiences that build a thriving aerial arts community.

Conclusion

In the next chapter, we'll explore marketing strategies that leverage your systems to attract ideal students and build lasting relationships with your community.

PART 3: GROWTH (Chapters 9-12)

→

Chapter 9

MARKETING THAT WORKS

> *"The best marketing doesn't feel like marketing - it feels like sharing something you're genuinely excited about with people who will love it as much as you do."* Nicola Ghalmi

The Fou

After growing Aerial Arts Academy to over 1000+ students across multiple venues, I've learned that sustainable marketing isn't about clever tactics or viral content. It's about consistently sharing your genuine passion for aerial arts with the right people in the right places. Your enthusiasm is contagious, and authentic excitement converts better than any sales script.

The most effective marketing strategies work because they're built on real relationships and genuine value. When students feel connected to your mission and see the transformation in themselves and others, they become your most powerful marketing asset. This chapter focuses on proven strategies that have driven our growth while maintaining the authentic community feel that makes aerial arts special.

Chapter 9

MARKETING THAT WORKS

Referral Programs That Actually Work

Our referral program succeeds because it's simple and valuable for everyone involved. Current students receive £10 credit for every successful referral that turns into a membership, while new students get their first class free with code OAA1STFREE. This creates a win-win situation where existing students save money while introducing friends to something they love.

Social Media Strategy That Builds Community

Social media for aerial studios isn't about perfection - it's about progress, community, and inspiration. Our content strategy focuses on student achievements, behind-the-scenes training moments, and educational content that showcases the accessibility and benefits of aerial arts. We use Social Pilot to maintain consistent posting while ensuring every piece of content aligns with our brand values.

Student spotlights (via IG reshare) generate the highest engagement because they're relatable and inspiring. We feature students of all levels celebrating achievements from first successful climb to advanced sequences. These posts demonstrate that aerial arts is for everyone while building individual confidence and community pride. Always get permission before featuring students, and focus on their journey rather than just the final result.

Educational content positions us as experts while providing value to followers who aren't yet students. Safety tips, beginner-friendly sequences, and myth-busting posts about aerial arts attract people researching the activity. This content builds trust and authority, making the transition from follower to student feel natural rather than sales-driven.

Chapter 9

MARKETING THAT WORKS

Email Marketing That Nurtures Relationships

Email marketing through Brevo allows us to maintain personal connections with our community while providing valuable content and timely information. Our email strategy focuses on three main types of content: educational resources, community updates, and exclusive offers for members.

New student welcome sequences introduce our community values, explain class progression, and provide helpful resources for getting started.

These automated emails reduce new student anxiety while building excitement for their aerial journey. The sequence includes safety reminders, what to expect in different class levels, and encouragement to ask questions.

Access your free subscripton to Aerial Studio Boost online for free resources

Chapter 9

MARKETING THAT WORKS

Email Marketing That Nurtures Relationships

Monthly newsletters celebrate student achievements, announce new classes or workshops, and share relevant fitness and wellness content. We include instructor spotlights, seasonal challenges, and behind-the-scenes content that makes subscribers feel part of an exclusive community.

The key is providing value in every email, not just promotional content. Segmented campaigns based on student behaviour and preferences increase engagement and conversion rates. Members receive different content than pay-as-you-go students, and inactive students get re-engagement campaigns with special offers.

This personalisation makes emails feel relevant rather than generic, improving open rates and reducing unsubscribes.

From : Aerial Arts Academy <info@aerialartsacademy.co.uk>
Reply : info@aerialartsacademy.co.uk
Subject : Jingle Bell Ball!

APPLY FOR A PERFORMER SLOT

We welcome any style of solo, doubles or group performance! Pole, Hoop, Silks, Heels, Acro, Burlesque... whatever your style, we welcome it!

Youth and Adult performers welcome!

There will be x 2 hoops/x2 silks available and x 2 45mm poles on the night. Spin or static, 1 or 2 apparatus can be used - YOUR CHOICE!

This evening is about YOU and our school and will be a relaxed and informal evening enabling you to showcase your passion and skills for fellow students and family in a supportive environment.

🎶 A no-pressure showcase to celebrate your success in a relaxed fun-filled evening!
🎶 Free practice sessions to support your routine!
🎶 Push yourself and explore performing!

date is set!

Jingle Bell Ball
Saturday December 6th, 6pm.
Oxford Academy.

This enchanting evening will feature captivating aerial routines where our students and teachers get to enjoy what they love together, making it a perfect way to celebrate the holiday season. Expect a range of Pole, Hoop, Silks, Heels and more!

Save the date for The Jingle Bell Ball and join us for an unforgettable evening filled with holiday cheer.

↻ Rotate

Chapter 9

Content Marketing That Educates and Inspires

Consistent content creation establishes expertise while providing value to current and potential students. Our blog covers topics from aerial arts benefits to injury prevention, creating resources that students share with friends and family. This content also improves our website's search engine visibility, attracting people researching aerial arts

Video content performs exceptionally well because it showcases the beauty and accessibility of aerial arts. We create beginner-friendly tutorials (on our hub), and student journey documentaries that inspire and educate. These videos work across multiple platforms - social media, website, and email campaigns - maximising content value.

User-generated content amplifies our marketing while building community pride. We encourage students to share their progress using studio hashtags and regularly feature their content on our channels. This approach provides authentic social proof while reducing content creation workload. Students love seeing their achievements celebrated, creating positive feedback loops that encourage continued sharing.

Chapter 9

MARKETING THAT WORKS

Measuring Marketing Success

Effective marketing requires tracking the right metrics to understand what's working and what needs adjustment. We monitor class booking sources, referral conversion rates, social media engagement, and email open rates to evaluate campaign effectiveness. Go Team Up's analytics help us understand which marketing channels drive the most valuable students.

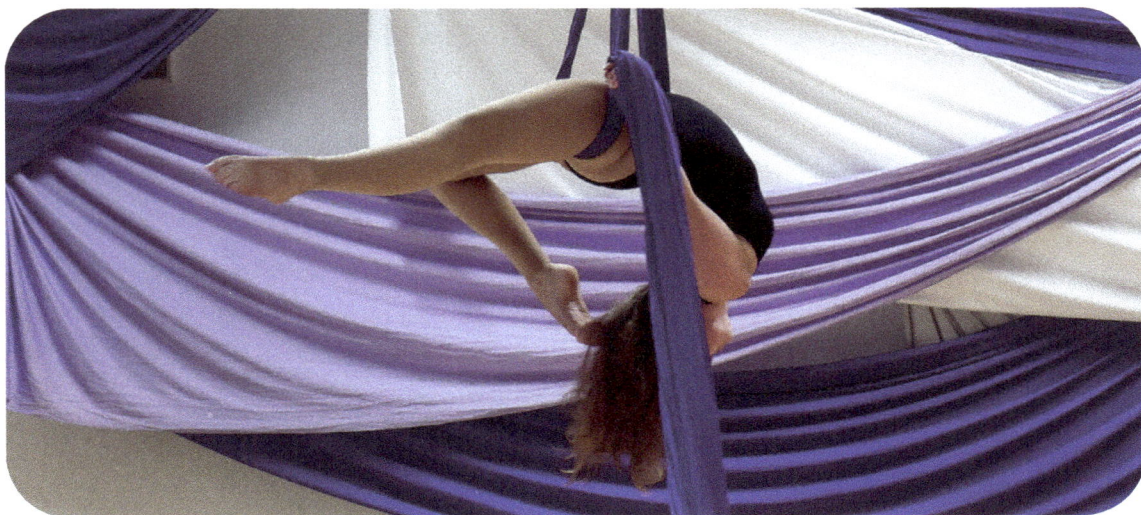

Customer lifetime value and retention rates are more important than initial acquisition costs. A marketing channel that brings students who stay for years is more valuable than one that generates quick sign-ups but poor retention. We track these metrics to focus resources on strategies that build long-term community rather than just short-term revenue.

Regular review and adjustment keep marketing efforts aligned with business goals and student needs. Monthly marketing meetings review performance data, discuss upcoming campaigns, and identify opportunities for improvement. This systematic approach ensures marketing efforts remain effective as the business grows and evolves.

Chapter 9

MARKETING THAT WORKS

Your Marketing Action Plan

Month 1: Foundation Building

☐ Set up referral program in Go Team Up with clear rewards structure

☐ Create Social Pilot account and develop content calendar

☐ Design email welcome sequence for new students in Brevo

☐ Identify local community events and partnership opportunities (for example we use cross marketing opportunities with Feel Fit Gym who are one of our venues)

☐ Establish brand voice and visual identity guidelines

☐ Create basic content templates for consistent messaging

Month 2: Content Creation and Community Building

☐ Develop library of educational content about aerial arts benefits

☐ Create student spotlight template and begin featuring achievements

☐ Launch monthly newsletter with community updates and tips

☐ Attend first local community event with promotional materials

Your Marketing Action Plan

☐ Begin user-generated content campaigns with branded hashtags

☐ Set up tracking systems for marketing performance metrics

Month 3: Optimisation and Expansion

☐ Analyse marketing performance data and identify top channels

☐ Refine email segmentation based on student behavior patterns

☐ Expand social media presence to additional relevant platforms

☐ Develop partnership agreements with complementary local businesses

☐ Create seasonal marketing campaigns aligned with business goals

☐ Plan advanced content like video tutorials and virtual studio tours

Ongoing: Consistency and Growth

☐ Maintain regular posting schedule across all marketing channels

☐ Monitor and respond to community engagement promptly

Ongoing: Consistency and Growth

☐ Continuously test and optimise email subject lines and content
☐ Seek new partnership and community engagement opportunities
☐ Track and celebrate marketing wins with team and community
☐ Adjust strategies based on performance data and student feedback

Marketing success comes from consistent effort, authentic messaging, and genuine care for your community. When your marketing feels like sharing something you love with people who will benefit, it stops being work and becomes a natural extension of your passion for aerial arts.

Conclusion

In the next chapter, we'll explore how to scale your operations while maintaining the quality and community feel that makes your studio special.

Chapter 10

DIVERSIFYING REVENUE

Multiple revenue streams create business stability and serve different customer needs. The key is developing offerings that complement your core classes while leveraging your existing expertise.

The Power of Revenue Diversification

Building multiple income streams protects your business from seasonal fluctuations and economic uncertainty. At Aerial Arts Academy, we've developed several complementary revenue sources that serve different customer segments while maximising our expertise and facility usage.

Private Lessons: Premium Personal Training

Private lessons at £35 for members and £45 for non-members provide personalised instruction for students needing individual attention. These sessions serve beginners who want confidence-building before group classes, advanced students working on specific skills, and anyone with scheduling constraints that don't align with regular class times.

The member discount reinforces membership value while the premium pricing reflects the true cost of one-on-one instruction. Private lessons also allow you to work with students who have injuries or physical limitations requiring modified approaches. This personalised service builds strong relationships and often leads to long-term membership commitments.

Group private options for two people at £60 for non-members and £50 for members provide a middle ground between group classes and individual instruction. These work well for friends wanting to learn together or couples seeking shared activities.

Chapter 10

DIVERSIFYING REVENUE

Workshop Development and Seasonal Themes

Internal workshops are included free for members as a value-add benefit, while non-members pay premium rates. We develop quarterly themed workshops around seasonal events - for example, Valentine's partner workshops, Halloween themed classes, and our annual Jingle Bell Ball celebration. These special events create excitement and give members exclusive access to unique experiences.

Workshop development allows you to explore specialised techniques, bring in guest instructors, and create memorable experiences that students share on social media. The seasonal approach ensures regular fresh content while building anticipation for upcoming events. These workshops also serve as excellent retention tools, giving members reasons to maintain their subscriptions.

Chapter 10

DIVERSIFYING REVENUE

The Aerial Education Hub: Digital Revenue Innovation

The Aerial Education Hub represents our most innovative revenue diversification - a comprehensive online platform providing our complete syllabus and class content. Originally created during COVID-19 lockdowns to maintain student engagement, the Hub has become a permanent value-add for all members.

The platform includes mini tutorials and full class videos, progression guides and conditioning and flexibility exercises, that students can access anytime. This digital resource serves multiple purposes: it provides value for members, creates passive income potential, and allows students to practice at home between classes. The Hub also positions us as industry experts, attracting students from beyond our local area.

What makes the Hub special is its integration with our physical classes. Students can review techniques before class, practice at home, and access advanced content as they progress. This blended approach enhances the learning experience while creating additional touchpoints with our brand.

The Hub operates as a separate subscription platform at £15/month, offering short tutorials and full classes in yoga, Pilates, heels, and aerial arts. However, all Aerial Arts Academy members receive free access as my "forever thank you" for their loyalty during the pandemic.

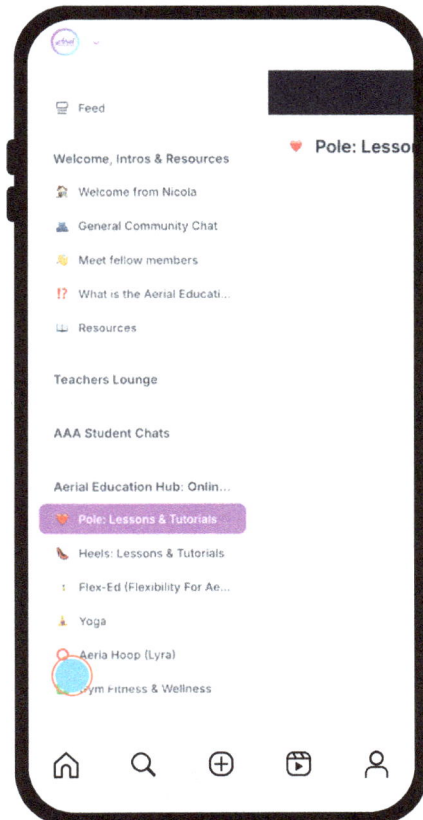

Chapter 10

DIVERSIFYING REVENUE

Additional Revenue Streams

Group parties for birthdays, hen dos, and corporate events utilise our facilities while introducing new people to aerial arts. These events often convert attendees into regular students while generating premium revenue from private group bookings.

Our annual Jingle Bell Ball and showcase events generate revenue through ticket sales and participant fees while building community.

Implementation Strategy

Start with one additional revenue stream and perfect it before adding others. Private lessons are often the easiest to implement since they require no additional equipment or scheduling complexity. Once established, workshops and parties can follow, with digital offerings like the Aerial Education Hub representing more advanced diversification.

The key is ensuring each revenue stream aligns with your brand values and serves your community's needs. Diversification should feel like natural extensions of your core offering rather than disconnected add-ons that dilute your focus. Here's our streams as an example

| Face-to-face fun tuition. Focused on community, safe teaching and progressive structure | Online fun tuition. Focused on community, safe teaching and progressive structure | Business & Marketing support for Aerial Studio owners that enables the creation of profitable thriving aerial communities |

Chapter 10

DIVERSIFYING REVENUE

Your Revenue Diversification Action Plan

Month 1: Private Lessons Launch

☐ Set up private lesson booking system in Go Team Up

☐ Create pricing structure

☐ Train instructors on private lesson delivery and internal process

☐ Develop marketing materials highlighting private lesson benefits

☐ Launch with existing students who've expressed interest

Month 2: Workshop Development

☐ Plan quarterly themed workshop calendar

☐ Create workshop content and pricing structure

☐ Set up member-exclusive booking system for free workshops

☐ Develop marketing campaigns for seasonal themes

☐ Host first workshop and gather feedback

Your Revenue Diversification Action Plan

Month 3: Party Services Launch

☐ Create party packages for birthdays, hen dos, and corporate events

☐ Develop pricing structure for private group bookings

☐ Train instructors on party delivery and group management

☐ Create marketing materials for party services

☐ Launch with promotional offers to existing students

Month 4: Digital Platform Development

☐ Research online platform options for online content delivery

☐ Create video content and digital resources

☐ Set up member access and content delivery system

☐ Integrate Hub access with membership benefits

☐ Launch with comprehensive member communication

Chapter 10

Ongoing: Optimisation and Growth

- ☐ Monitor revenue performance across all streams
- ☐ Gather customer feedback and adjust offerings
- ☐ Develop seasonal campaigns and special events
- ☐ Explore additional opportunities like corporate wellness
- ☐ Track customer lifetime value across different services

Revenue diversification isn't about adding complexity - it's about serving your community's varied needs while building business resilience. Each additional stream should strengthen your core offering while providing new ways for students to engage with your brand.

Conclusion

In the next chapter, we'll explore scaling strategies that maintain quality while expanding your reach and impact.

Chapter 11

BUILDING COMMUNITY

A strong community isn't built overnight - it's cultivated through consistent care, shared experiences, and genuine connections. Here's how to create a studio culture that keeps students coming back for years.

Why Community Matters More Than Classes

When students join Aerial Arts Academy, they're not just signing up for fitness classes - they're joining a community. After growing to over 1000+ students across multiple venues, I've learned that technical instruction alone doesn't create lasting businesses. Students stay for the relationships, the support, and the sense of belonging they find within your studio walls.

Community building is your most powerful retention tool. Students who feel connected to your studio culture are more likely to attend regularly, refer friends, and continue their membership even during challenging times. The investment in community pays dividends through reduced churn, increased lifetime value, and organic growth through word-of-mouth referrals.

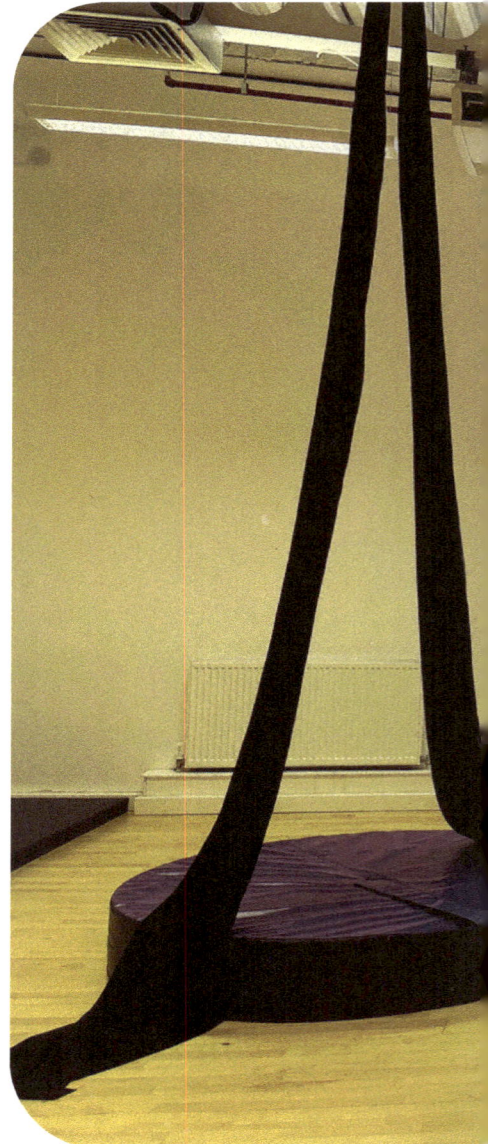

Chapter 11

BUILDING COMMUNITY

Member Retention Strategies That Work

Retention starts from the moment a student walks through your door. The first few classes are critical - students who feel welcomed, supported, and successful in their initial experiences are far more likely to become long-term members. This is why we focus intensively on the new student experience, ensuring every interaction reinforces their decision to join our community.

The First 30 Days: New students receive extra attention during their first month. Instructors learn their names quickly, check in on their progress, and provide encouragement when they struggle. We celebrate small wins - their first successful climb, holding a pose for the first time, or simply showing up consistently. These early positive experiences create emotional connections that transcend the physical workout.

Progress Recognition: Students need to see and feel their improvement to stay motivated. We use level progression systems, achievement certificates, and public recognition to highlight student growth. When someone masters a challenging sequence or reaches a new level, we celebrate it publicly through social media (with permission), in-class announcements, and our newsletters. This recognition motivates the individual while inspiring others.

Chapter 11

BUILDING COMMUNITY

Flexible Policies: Life happens, and rigid policies drive students away. We offer membership freezes for injuries, travel, or life changes. Class credits are often allowed to roll over within reasonable timeframes. We work with students facing financial difficulties rather than immediately canceling memberships. This flexibility shows we care about people, not just revenue.

Event Planning: The Jingle Bell Ball Success Story

Our annual Jingle Bell Ball exemplifies how events build community while generating revenue. This end-of-year celebration brings together students, instructors, friends, and family for performances, socialising, and shared achievement. The event serves multiple purposes: showcasing student progress, building community bonds, and creating memorable experiences that strengthen studio loyalty.

Planning Process: Event planning begins months in advance with theme selection, venue booking, and performance preparation.

Performance Opportunities: Students of all levels can participate, from beginners performing simple sequences to advanced students showcasing complex routines - even our youth athletes are invited to join. The emphasis is on personal achievement rather than perfection. Watching fellow students perform builds appreciation for everyone's journey and creates supportive audience dynamics.

Chapter 11

BUILDING COMMUNITY

Community Celebration:
The Jingle Bell Ball includes social time and opportunities for students to connect outside the class environment. These interactions strengthen relationships and create the social bonds that keep people engaged with your studio long-term.

Revenue Generation:
While community building is the primary goal, events also generate revenue through ticket sales, participant fees, and merchandise.

The financial success helps fund future events while demonstrating the commercial value of community investment.

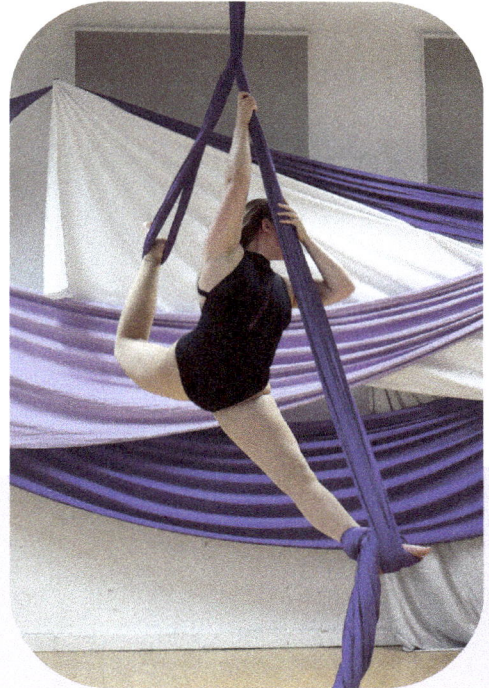

Creating Member Loyalty and Engagement

Loyalty isn't bought - it's earned through consistent positive experiences and genuine care for your students' success. Building loyalty requires understanding what motivates different students and creating multiple ways for them to feel valued and connected to your community.

Exclusive Member Benefits: Members receive access to free workshops, priority booking, free open training sessions, discounted private lessons, and exclusive events. These benefits create tangible value while making members feel special and appreciated.

Chapter 11

BUILDING COMMUNITY

Student Advisory:

Involving students in studio decisions creates investment in outcomes. We regularly survey members about class preferences, schedule changes, and new program ideas. Student feedback directly influences our programming, making members feel heard and valued.

Milestone Celebrations:

Recognising membership anniversaries, achievement milestones, and personal accomplishments shows students that their journey matters to you. Simple gestures like anniversary cards, achievement certificates, or social media shout-outs create emotional connections that strengthen loyalty.

Peer Support Systems:

Encouraging students to support each other creates a self-sustaining community culture. Advanced students mentor beginners, study groups form around challenging skills, and friendships develop through shared experiences. This peer support reduces instructor workload while strengthening community bonds.

Building a Studio Culture

Culture isn't what you say - it's what you consistently do. Your studio culture is created through daily interactions, policy decisions, and the behavior you model and reward. Building positive culture requires intentional effort and consistent reinforcement of your values.

Chapter 11

BUILDING COMMUNITY

Values in Action:

Our core values of safety, inclusivity, and personal growth guide every decision. When policies conflict with values, we adjust policies. When behavior doesn't align with values, we address it immediately. Students learn your true values through your actions, not your marketing materials.

Instructor Culture:

Your team creates the daily culture students experience. Hiring instructors who embody your values, training them on community building, and recognising positive cultural contributions ensures consistent experiences across all classes and venues.

Physical Environment:

Your studio space should reflect your culture. Welcoming décor, inspirational messages, student achievement displays, and comfortable social areas all contribute to the atmosphere you're creating. Students should feel the culture the moment they walk in.

Communication Style:

How you communicate - in person, online, and in writing - shapes culture. We maintain a positive, encouraging tone that celebrates effort over perfection. Our language emphasises growth, support, and community rather than competition or judgment.

Chapter 11

BUILDING COMMUNITY

Measuring Community Health

Retention Metrics:
Track membership retention rates, class attendance patterns, and student longevity.

Declining metrics often indicate community health issues that need attention.

Engagement Indicators:
Monitor social media engagement, event attendance, referral rates, and student feedback. High engagement suggests strong community bonds, while declining participation may signal cultural problems.

Qualitative Feedback:
Regular student surveys, informal conversations, and instructor observations provide insights into community health that numbers can't capture. Students will tell you when something feels off - listen to them.

Your Community Building Action Plan

Month 1: Foundation Setting

☐ Define your studio values and culture goals
☐ Train instructors on community building techniques
☐ Implement new student welcome procedures
☐ Create member recognition systems
☐ Plan first quarterly community event

Month 2: Engagement Systems

☐ Launch student advisory group or feedback system
☐ Implement progress tracking and celebration procedures
☐ Create exclusive member benefits program
☐ Develop social media community engagement strategy
☐ Plan seasonal workshop or challenge program

Month 3: Event Planning

☐ Plan major annual event (like Jingle Bell Ball)
☐ Create event planning committee with student volunteers
☐ Develop event marketing and promotion strategy
☐ Set up performance preparation and support systems
☐ Plan community celebration elements

Ongoing: Culture Maintenance

☐ Regularly assess community health through metrics and feedback

☐ Adjust policies and procedures to support community goals

☐ Recognise and reward positive community contributions

☐ Address cultural issues quickly and directly

☐ Continuously invest in instructor development and team culture

Building community takes time, but the investment pays dividends through increased retention, organic growth, and a more fulfilling business experience. When students feel genuinely connected to your studio and each other, they become advocates who help your business thrive while creating the supportive environment that makes aerial arts transformational.

Conclusion

In the next chapter, we'll explore scaling strategies that allow you to grow your business while maintaining the community culture that makes it special.

Chapter 12

SCALING & FRANCHISING

Scaling isn't just about getting bigger - it's about creating systems that can replicate your success while maintaining the quality and culture that made you successful in the first place.

The Franchise Vision

When I started Aerial Arts Academy, I never imagined it would grow to over 1000 students across multiple venues. But as the business evolved and systems matured, I began to see the potential for franchising. My goal is to secure two franchises year-on-year, not just for financial growth, but to share the transformational power of aerial arts with more communities.

Franchising represents the ultimate test of your business systems. If you can teach someone else to replicate your success in a different location, you've built something truly scalable.

The franchise model creates win-win relationships where success is shared while allowing for rapid growth with less capital investment.

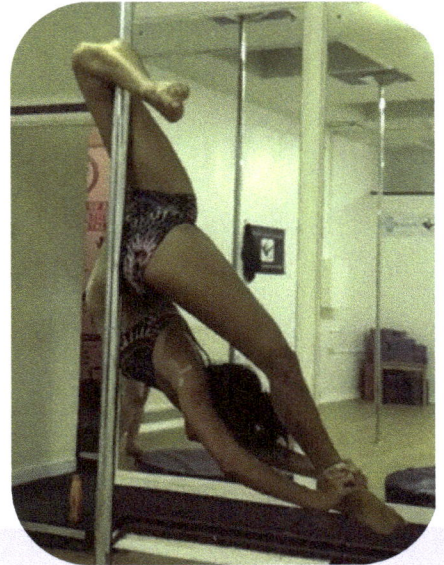

Access your free subscripton to Aerial Studio Boost online for free resources

Chapter 12
SCALING & FRANCHISING

Why Franchise Instead of Company-Owned Expansion

After running multiple venues myself, I've learned that local ownership often produces better results than remote management. Franchise partners bring local market knowledge, personal investment, and entrepreneurial drive that employed managers rarely match. They understand their communities in ways that distant owners cannot.

Franchising also provides faster expansion with less capital investment. Instead of funding each new location myself, franchise partners provide the initial investment while I contribute the proven systems and ongoing support. When franchisees succeed, the entire network grows stronger.

Franchise Development Goals and Strategies

My specific goal of two franchises year-on-year reflects realistic growth that allows for proper support and system refinement. Rapid expansion often leads to quality issues and franchise partner dissatisfaction. Starting with two locations allows me to perfect the franchise model before broader expansion.

Ideal franchise partners combine business experience with passion for aerial arts. They need sufficient capital for startup costs, understanding of local markets, and commitment to maintaining our quality standards. Former students who've experienced our culture often make excellent franchise candidates.

Initial franchise locations should be far enough from existing venues to avoid market overlap but close enough for regular support visits. This geographic approach allows for regional brand building while maintaining operational efficiency.

Chapter 12

SCALING & FRANCHISING

Systems Replication and Standardisation

Every aspect of running an Aerial Arts Academy must be documented in detail. From class structures and safety protocols to marketing strategies and customer service standards, the operations manual becomes the blueprint for franchise success.

Go Team Up, Brevo, and Social Pilot integrations must be standardised across all locations. Franchise partners receive pre-configured systems that match our proven setup, ensuring consistency while reducing their learning curve. The 10-week instructor training program becomes even more critical in franchise locations, ensuring quality consistency across all venues.

Brand standards covering visual identity, communication style, and customer experience must remain consistent across all locations. Regular audits, mystery shopper programs, and performance metrics ensure franchise locations maintain our standards while providing improvement feedback.

Chapter 12

SCALING & FRANCHISING

The Aerial Education Hub Advantage

Our online platform provides significant competitive advantages for franchise development. The Hub offers immediate value to new franchise locations, providing content and resources that would take years to develop independently. This digital asset differentiates our franchise opportunity from competitors.

Franchise partners can offer Hub access to their members immediately, providing premium value that justifies membership pricing. The platform also enables consistent training and ongoing education across all locations, maintaining quality standards regardless of geographic distance.

Expansion Planning and Execution

Each potential franchise location requires thorough market analysis including demographics, competition, venue availability, and local regulations. The partner selection process evaluates financial capacity, relevant experience, cultural fit, and local market knowledge.

New franchise locations receive intensive support during their first 90 days including site setup assistance, staff training, marketing launch support, and regular check-ins to address challenges quickly. Ongoing support through regular training updates, marketing assistance, and operational guidance ensures continued success.

Access your free subscripton to Aerial Studio Boost online for free resources

Chapter 12

SCALING & FRANCHISING

Growth Management and Quality Control

Key performance indicators track franchise location success including membership growth, retention rates, safety incidents, and customer satisfaction.

Clear policies and procedures for addressing franchise partner concerns, territory disputes, and performance issues protect both the network and individual partners. Fair, consistent application of these policies maintains network integrity while supporting struggling locations.

Financial and Legal Considerations

Initial franchise fees must reflect the value provided while remaining accessible to qualified partners. Monthly royalty payments support ongoing franchise support, system development, and brand marketing. The royalty structure must balance network support needs with franchise partner profitability. Go Team Up offers a franchise facility so you can monitor all franchise payments and infrastructure.

Legal requirements include detailed disclosure documents, territory rights definition, intellectual property protection, and compliance monitoring. These elements must be prepared by qualified franchise attorneys and updated regularly to protect both the network and individual partners.

Chapter 12

Your Franchise Development Action Plan

Months 1-3: Foundation Building

☐ Complete comprehensive operations manual documentation

☐ Develop franchise partner profile and selection criteria

☐ Create financial projections and fee structure

☐ Begin legal documentation with franchise attorney

☐ Identify potential franchise territories and markets

Months 4-6: System Standardization

☐ Standardise all technology systems for franchise deployment

☐ Create franchise training programs and materials

☐ Develop quality control and monitoring systems

☐ Begin franchise partner recruitment and screening

Months 7-9: Partner Selection and Training

☐ Complete franchise partner selection process

☐ Conduct intensive franchise partner training

☐ Assist with site selection and setup

☐ Implement technology systems at franchise locations

Your Franchise Development Action Plan

Months 10-12: Launch and Optimisation
☐ Launch first franchise locations with full support
☐ Monitor performance and provide ongoing assistance
☐ Gather feedback and refine franchise systems
☐ Begin recruitment for second franchise location
Ongoing: Network Management
☐ Maintain regular communication with franchise partners
☐ Monitor performance and provide improvement support
☐ Continue system development and updates
☐ Expand network through additional franchise sales

Your Franchise Development Action Plan

Franchising represents the ultimate expression of business systematisation. When you can teach others to replicate your success, you've created something that transcends individual effort and becomes a lasting contribution to your industry and community.

The goal isn't just to grow bigger - it's to create a network of successful business owners who share your passion for aerial arts while building thriving businesses that transform lives in their communities.

Conclusion

This concludes Part 3: Growth.

In the final section, we'll explore common challenges solved, round up of the key takeaways learned form my journey, the future of aerial arts and of course your next steps to make your own studio thrive (with profitability - but without burning out!)

PART 4: REAL-WORLD CASE STUDIES (Chapters 13-15)

CHAPTER 13: MY JOURNEY

CHAPTER 14: COMMON CHALLENGES SOLVED

CHAPTER 15: THE FUTURE OF AERIAL ARTS

→

Chapter 13

MY JOURNEY

Every successful business has a story behind it - the real story of challenges overcome, lessons learned, and pivotal moments that shaped everything that followed. This is mine.

The Beginning: From Acquisition to Innovation

My journey into the aerial arts business world began when I purchased Dance Inspires, Oxford's first pole dance school. Taking over an existing business taught me immediately that ownership brings both opportunities and inherited challenges. While I gained an established brand and some existing students, I also inherited operational issues and systems that needed significant improvement.

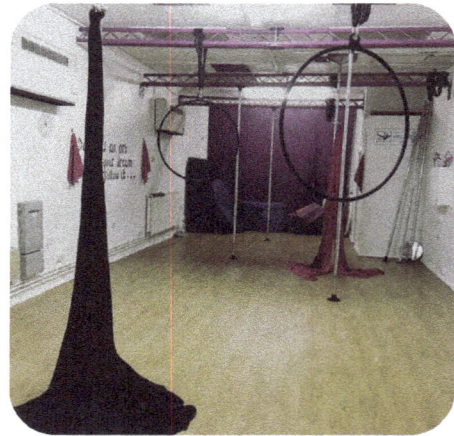

The experience of buying and running Dance Inspires was my introduction to the realities of studio ownership. I learned about venue management, instructor relationships, and the constant balance between maintaining quality and controlling costs. What seemed like a straightforward acquisition quickly became a masterclass in business problem-solving.

The challenges were immediate and significant. The studio was locked into a traditional lease with a difficult landlord, creating ongoing stress like roofing leads and financial pressure. Managing inherited staff, maintaining student satisfaction, and trying to improve profitability while dealing with venue issues proved more complex than I'd anticipated.

The Dance Inspires Experience: Hard Lessons Learned

Running Dance Inspires taught me that buying a business doesn't mean buying success - it means buying problems to solve. The most significant challenge was our venue situation. The traditional lease created enormous financial pressure, and the landlord relationship deteriorated to the point where it affected everything from class scheduling to student confidence in our stability.

I learned that venue partnerships are crucial business relationships that can make or break your studio. When the landlord relationship became untenable, it impacted every aspect of operations. The stress of managing a failing lease while trying to maintain quality instruction and student satisfaction was overwhelming.

Eventually, Dance Inspires was forced to close when we were evicted from our premises, which were later converted to flats. While devastating at the time, this experience taught me invaluable lessons about risk management, the importance of flexible venue arrangements, and the need for multiple contingency plans.

The financial loss was significant, but the education was priceless. I learned that traditional leases create enormous risk for studios, that landlord relationships require as much attention as customer relationships, and that having backup plans isn't pessimistic - it's essential. Most importantly, I learned that sometimes the best business decision is knowing when to walk away and start fresh.

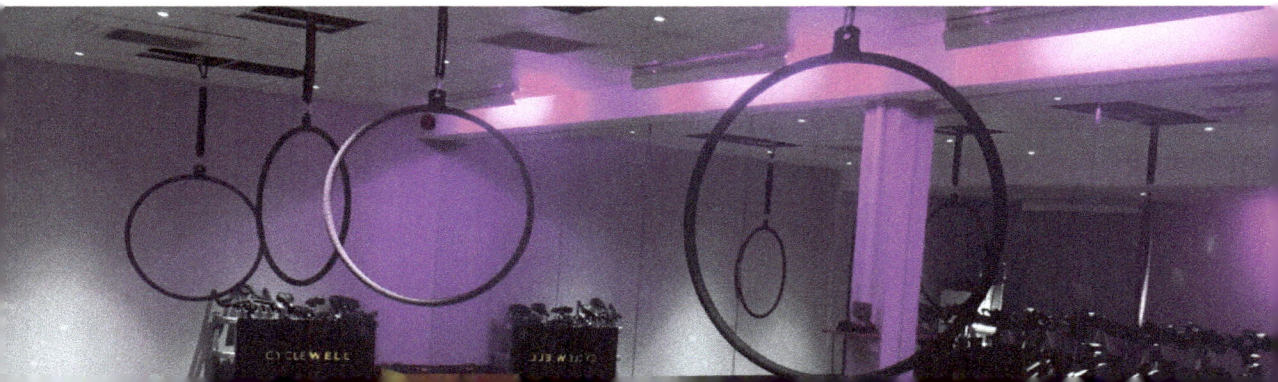

Chapter 13

MY JOURNEY

The Phoenix Rises: Launching Aerial Arts Academy (2019)

When I decided to start fresh with Aerial Arts Academy in 2019 (after selling Dance Inspires - do I regret that sale? yes and no... but that's a whole story in itself!), I was determined to apply everything I'd learned from the Dance Inspires experience. This time, I would build from the ground up with systems, flexibility, and risk management as core principles from day one.

Instead of committing to expensive leases, I negotiated hourly venue rentals at Oxford Academy and Feel Fit Gym. This approach provided flexibility and dramatically reduced financial risk.

The launch strategy was completely different from my Dance Inspires experience. I focused on building systems from day one, implementing Go Team Up for bookings, and creating standardised processes that could scale. The 10-week instructor training program ensured quality consistency, while the self-employed contractor model provided flexibility for both the business and instructors.

The COVID-19 Pivot: Innovation Through Necessity (April 2020)

In April 2020, just as Aerial Arts Academy was gaining momentum after just a few months,, COVID-19 lockdowns forced us to close. Instead of seeing this as a disaster, I viewed it as an opportunity to innovate. Within a few days, we'd transitioned to online classes via Zoom and I started to creat the Aerial Education Hub which I launched within 1 month - a comprehensive digital platform providing our complete syllabus and class content.

The remarkable thing was that we didn't lose a single member during lockdown. Students appreciated our quick adaptation and continued engagement. The online platform became so valuable that when we reopened, I decided to provide free Hub access to all members as my "forever thank you" for their loyalty during the pandemic.

This experience taught me that adaptability and innovation often emerge from challenges. The Aerial Education Hub, born from necessity during those early pandemic months, became one of our most valuable assets and a significant differentiator in the market.

Chapter 13

MY JOURNEY

Key Milestones and Turning Points

→ **2006:** Purchased Dance Inspires, learning the complexities of business acquisition and inherited challenges.

→ **2019:** Launched Aerial Arts Academy with a completely different business model focused on venue partnerships and systematic growth.

→ **April 2020:** COVID-19 lockdown forces closure, but we pivot to online delivery within days, maintaining our entire membership base.

→ **Summer 2020:** Reopening with enhanced safety protocols and the new Aerial Education Hub as a permanent member benefit.

→ **2021-2022:** Expansion to multiple venues and growth to over 500 members, proving the scalability of our venue partnership model.

→ **2023:** Reaching 700 members and establishing ourselves as Oxford's premier aerial arts destination.

→ **2024:** Continued growth to over 1000 students across multiple venues, with plans for franchise development.

Each milestone represented not just numerical growth, but proof that the systems and strategies developed through hard experience were working. The contrast between the struggles of Dance Inspires and the steady growth of Aerial Arts Academy validated every lesson learned.

Chapter 13

MY JOURNEY

Financial Growth Trajectory

The financial journey from Dance Inspires to Aerial Arts Academy illustrates the importance of sustainable business models. Dance Inspires struggled with high fixed costs and inflexible arrangements that made profitability difficult even with decent student numbers.

Aerial Arts Academy's financial model, based on flexible venue costs and scalable systems, created a completely different trajectory. The hourly venue rentals meant costs scaled with revenue, providing natural cash flow management. The membership model created predictable recurring revenue, while private lessons and workshops provided additional income streams.

The key financial turning point came when we reached approximately 75 members - the point where membership revenue consistently covered all fixed costs. Beyond this threshold, additional members contributed directly to profitability, creating the foundation for sustainable growth and eventual franchise development.

Today, with over 1000+ students and multiple revenue streams, the business generates the financial stability that allows me to focus on growth and innovation rather than survival. The contrast with Dance Inspires couldn't be more stark.

Chapter 13

MY JOURNEY

Pivotal Decisions That Changed Everything

Learning from Dance Inspires and Starting Fresh: Rather than trying to fix inherited problems, I chose to start over with better foundations.

Choosing Venue Partnerships Over Leases: This single decision eliminated the primary risk that destroyed Dance Inspires while providing access to better facilities than I could afford independently.

Implementing Systems From Day One: Rather than growing organically and adding systems later, I built Aerial Arts Academy on systematic foundations that could scale efficiently.

The Self-Employed Instructor Model: This approach provided flexibility while reducing administrative burden and financial risk.

Creating the Aerial Education Hub During COVID: What started as a pandemic response became a permanent competitive advantage and member benefit.

Focusing on Community Building: Recognising that retention matters more than acquisition led to strategies that created lasting student relationships.

Personal Growth and Leadership Development

The journey from buying Dance Inspires to building Aerial Arts Academy required developing leadership skills I didn't know I needed. The experience of managing an acquired business versus building from scratch taught me different aspects of entrepreneurship.

With Dance Inspires, I learned about inheriting problems, managing existing relationships, and making difficult decisions about when to persist versus when to pivot. With Aerial Arts Academy, I learned about building culture, establishing systems, and creating sustainable growth from the ground up.

Chapter 13

MY JOURNEY

The COVID-19 pivot particularly tested my leadership abilities. Making quick decisions under pressure, maintaining team morale during uncertainty, and innovating solutions while supporting anxious students required skills I'd never needed before. The experience proved that effective leadership often emerges from necessity rather than planning.

Perhaps most importantly, I learned that vulnerability and authenticity create stronger connections than trying to appear perfect. Sharing challenges with students and staff built trust and community in ways that polished presentations never could.

The Franchise Vision Emerges

As Aerial Arts Academy stabilised and grew, I began to see possibilities beyond a single studio. The systems we'd developed, the community we'd built, and the lessons we'd learned represented value that could benefit other communities.

The upcoming franchise vision isn't about rapid expansion or maximising revenue - it's about sharing what works while supporting other passionate individuals who want to build their own aerial arts communities. The goal of two franchises by year-on-year represents careful, sustainable growth that maintains quality while extending our impact.

Looking Back: What I Wish I'd Known

If I could go back and advise myself when purchasing Dance Inspires, I'd emphasise the importance of thoroughly understanding inherited risks, especially venue arrangements. I'd also stress the value of having exit strategies and contingency plans from day one.

Chapter 13

MY JOURNEY

For launching Aerial Arts Academy, I'd emphasize that starting fresh with the right foundations is often better than trying to fix inherited problems. The technical aspects of aerial arts instruction were never the challenge - it was the business fundamentals that required the steepest learning curve.

Most importantly, I'd emphasise that setbacks aren't failures - they're education. The lessons learned from Dance Inspires' challenges became the foundation for Aerial Arts Academy's success. Every difficult experience contributed to the knowledge that now helps others avoid similar pitfalls.

The Journey Continues

Today, as I work toward franchise development and continue growing Aerial Arts Academy, I'm grateful for every part of the journey - including the painful lessons from Dance Inspires and the unexpected challenges of the pandemic. The combination of acquisition experience, startup creation, crisis management, and systematic thinking has created something sustainable and scalable.

The story isn't finished. Each new student, instructor, and potential franchise partner adds new chapters to this ongoing journey. What started as purchasing a small pole dance school has evolved into a mission to help others build their own successful studios.

This journey from business acquisition through closure to startup success and pandemic adaptation proves that with the right approach, persistence, and willingness to learn from mistakes, it's possible to build something meaningful and profitable in the aerial arts industry.

Conclusion

In the next chapter, we'll explore the common challenges that every studio owner faces and the practical solutions that have proven effective in real-world situations.

Chapter 14

COMMON CHALLENGES SOLVED

Every studio owner faces similar challenges - the difference between success and failure lies in how quickly you recognize problems and implement effective solutions. Here are the real challenges I've faced and the practical solutions that actually work.

The Reality of Studio Ownership

Running an aerial arts studio sounds glamorous from the outside - teaching something you love, building community, helping people transform their lives. The reality includes dealing with difficult customers, managing instructor drama, handling equipment failures, and solving problems you never anticipated. And that's all before soreness from actually teaching!! IYKYK!! Success comes from developing systems to handle these challenges efficiently rather than hoping they won't occur.

I've encountered virtually every challenge a studio owner can face. Some problems have obvious solutions, others require creative thinking, and a few demand difficult decisions. The key is learning from each challenge to prevent similar issues in the future.

Chapter 14

COMMON CHALLENGES SOLVED

Instructor Management Challenges

Challenge: Inconsistent Teaching Quality Different instructors naturally have different teaching styles, but inconsistent safety standards or progression methods confuse students and create liability risks. I discovered this when students complained about conflicting instruction between classes.

Solution: Standardised Training Program Our 10-week instructor training program covers not just aerial techniques but teaching methodology, safety protocols, and customer service standards. Every instructor receives the same foundation training, ensuring consistency across all classes. Regular refresher sessions and peer observations maintain standards over time. We also use a student progression chart to ensure that the team are teaching levels consistently.

Challenge: Instructor Reliability Issues Instructors calling in sick at the last minute, showing up late, or canceling classes creates operational chaos and disappoints students. This is unavoidable, but you just need a contingency that allows for substitutes!

Solution: Clear Expectations and Backup Systems We established clear policies about notice periods for cancellations, punctuality requirements, and professional standards. More importantly, we developed backup instructor systems where qualified team members can cover classes at short notice. Cross-training instructors on multiple disciplines provides flexibility when coverage is needed.

Challenge: Managing Self-Employed Contractors Balancing the need for consistency with the legal requirements of self-employed status creates ongoing tension. Instructors want flexibility, but the business needs reliability and quality control.

Solution: Clear Contractor Agreements Our contractor agreements clearly define expectations while respecting self-employed status. We provide guidelines rather than rigid rules, focusing on outcomes rather than methods. Regular communication and feedback sessions maintain relationships while ensuring standards are met.

Chapter 14

COMMON CHALLENGES SOLVED

Customer Retention Issues

Challenge: New Student Dropout Many students attend a few classes then disappear, often because they feel overwhelmed, intimidated, or unsure about their progress. This was particularly noticeable in our early days when we lacked structured onboarding.

Solution: Comprehensive New Student Experience We created a structured welcome process including pre-class communication, personalised attention during first classes, and follow-up contact after initial sessions. The free first class with code OAA1STFREE removes initial barriers, while our level progression system helps students see their advancement clearly.

Challenge: Seasonal Membership Fluctuations January brings New Year resolution members who often quit by March. Summer sees reduced attendance as people travel or focus on outdoor activities. These fluctuations made financial planning difficult.

Solution: Flexible Membership Options and Seasonal Programming We offer membership freezes for travel or temporary life changes, reducing cancellations. Seasonal programming like summer intensives and winter workshops maintains engagement year-round. The Aerial Education Hub provides value even when students can't attend physical classes.

Challenge: Managing Complex Customer Situations Occasionally, challenging situations arise that require careful handling - from disagreements about policies to requests for special accommodations due to life circumstances. These situations test your ability to maintain fairness while preserving relationships and studio harmony.

Solution: Clear Policies with Flexible Application We established comprehensive studio policies that cover common scenarios while maintaining flexibility for genuine hardships. Staff training includes conflict resolution techniques and escalation procedures to handle sensitive situations professionally. Most importantly, we address concerns promptly and privately, focusing on finding mutually acceptable solutions that maintain goodwill while protecting studio standards.

Chapter 14

COMMON CHALLENGES SOLVED

Operational Hurdles and Resolutions

Challenge: Equipment Maintenance and Safety Aerial equipment requires regular inspection and maintenance to ensure safety. Equipment failures during classes create safety risks and disrupt operations. Initially, I underestimated the time and cost involved in proper equipment management.

Solution: Systematic Maintenance Schedules We implemented regular equipment inspection schedules with detailed checklists. All staff are trained to identify potential issues and report them immediately. We maintain backup equipment for critical items and have established relationships with reliable suppliers for quick replacements.

Challenge: Venue Coordination Across Multiple Locations Managing classes at Oxford Academy, Leys Leisure Centre, Feel Fit Gym and our full time Witney venue requires coordination of schedules, equipment transport, and different venue requirements. Double-bookings or equipment shortages can ruin classes.

Solution: Centralised Scheduling and Equipment Management Go Team Up manages all venue bookings from a single system, preventing conflicts. We maintain equipment sets at each venue to minimise transport requirements. Clear communication protocols with venue managers ensure smooth operations.

Challenge: Managing Growth Without Losing Quality As we expanded from 75 to over 1000 students, maintaining the personal touch and quality standards became increasingly difficult. Students complained about feeling lost in larger classes or not receiving individual attention.

Solution: Scalable Systems with Personal Touch We maintained maximum class sizes (15 students for group classes) while adding more class times rather than larger classes. Instructor training emphasises personal connection and individual attention. The member recognition systems ensure students feel valued regardless of studio size.

Chapter 14

COMMON CHALLENGES SOLVED

Technology and Systems Challenges

Challenge: Booking System Limitations Our initial manual booking system (at Dance Inspires) quickly became unmanageable. Students couldn't book online, payment processing was manual, and class management was chaotic.

Solution: Comprehensive Platform Integration Implementing BookWhen solved many of these problems. At Aerial Arts Academy i transitioned to Go Team Up for its far superior features - online booking, payment processing, membership management, and communication. The system scales with growth while maintaining functionality. Integration with other tools like Brevo for email marketing creates a seamless experience.

Challenge: Communication Overload As membership grew, individual communication became impossible while mass communication felt impersonal. Students missed important information or felt overwhelmed by messages.

Solution: Segmented Communication Strategy We use Brevo to segment communications based on membership type, class preferences, and engagement levels. Automated sequences handle routine communications while personal messages address individual needs. The balance maintains efficiency while preserving personal connection. SMS and Whatsapp campaigns helped us to develop quick communication tactics.

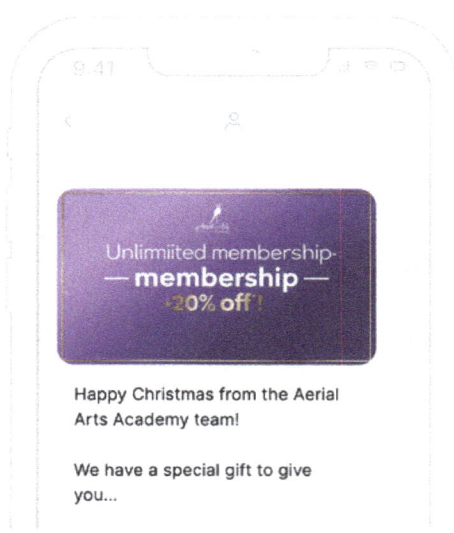

WE HAVE 2 PERFORMER SLOTS LEFT for the Jingle Bell Ball ❄ Dec 7, 6PM @OX4

This magical evening will showcase mesmerising aerial performances, allowing our students and teachers to share their passion together, creating an

Unlimiited membership-
— membership —
-20% off !

Happy Christmas from the Aerial Arts Academy team!

We have a special gift to give you...

140

Chapter 14

COMMON CHALLENGES SOLVED

Financial Management Challenges

Challenge: Cash Flow Fluctuations Seasonal membership changes, unexpected expenses, and irregular workshop income created cash flow challenges. The hourly venue rental model helped but didn't eliminate financial uncertainty.

Solution: Diversified Revenue Streams and Financial Planning Multiple revenue sources (memberships, private lessons, workshops, parties, Aerial Education Hub) provide stability. Monthly financial reviews track trends and identify potential issues early. Maintaining operating reserves helps manage unexpected expenses or revenue dips.

Challenge: Pricing Strategy Complexity Balancing competitive pricing with profitability while maintaining perceived value requires constant adjustment. Member versus non-member pricing, workshop fees, and private lesson rates all impact overall profitability.

Solution: Data-Driven Pricing Decisions We regularly analyse competitor pricing, student feedback, and financial performance to optimise pricing. The membership structure (£40-£154 monthly) provides options for different budgets while encouraging higher-value commitments. Regular pricing reviews ensure we remain competitive while maintaining margins.

Access your free subscripton to Aerial Studio Boost online for free resources

Chapter 14

COMMON CHALLENGES SOLVED

Prevention Strategies

Regular Review Systems: Daily team updatesidentify emerging issues before they become serious problems. A Whatsapp instructor group is used for quick comms. Student feedback surveys provide early warning about potential challenges.

Clear Communication Channels: Students and staff know how to raise concerns and can expect timely responses. Open communication prevents small issues from becoming major problems.

Continuous Training: Regular staff training on new procedures, safety updates, and customer service maintains standards as the business grows.

Financial Monitoring: Monthly financial reviews track key metrics and identify trends that might indicate emerging challenges.

Your Challenge Prevention Toolkit

Monthly Review Checklist

☐ Analyse student retention and identify any concerning trends

☐ Review instructor performance and address any issues

☐ Check equipment condition and schedule maintenance

☐ Assess financial performance against targets

☐ Gather student feedback through surveys or informal conversations

☐ Review operational procedures and identify improvements

Crisis Management Procedures

☐ Establish clear escalation procedures for different types of problems

☐ Create backup plans for common issues (instructor illness, equipment failure)

☐ Maintain emergency contact lists for key suppliers and services

Chapter 14

Your Challenge Prevention Toolkit

☐ Document solutions to recurring problems for future reference

☐ Train staff on crisis response procedures

Growth Management Systems

☐ Set maximum class sizes and stick to them

☐ Plan instructor recruitment ahead of capacity needs

☐ Regularly review and update training programs

☐ Monitor customer satisfaction as you scale

☐ Maintain financial reserves for unexpected challenges

The key to managing challenges is expecting them and having systems in place to address them quickly. Every problem is an opportunity to improve your operations and prevent similar issues in the future.

The studios that thrive are those that learn from challenges rather than being defeated by them.

Your Challenge Prevention Toolkit

Conclusion

In the next chapter, we'll explore the future of aerial arts and the opportunities that lie ahead for studio owners who are ready to embrace change and innovation.

Keep reading on for your 30 day → 2 → 5 year action plan!

Chapter 15

THE FUTURE OF AERIAL ARTS

The aerial arts industry is evolving rapidly, creating new opportunities for studio owners who are ready to embrace change and innovation. Here's where the industry is heading and how to position your studio for future success.

THE EVOLUTION OF AERIAL ARTS

When I first entered the aerial arts world, pole dancing was still fighting stigma and aerial hoop was considered a niche skill. In fact, pole in particular was developed by strippers and sex workers! Our industry tries to cover up this fact, but as studio owners, it is our responsibility to ensure that we respect the true heritage of pole.

Today, aerial arts has exploded into mainstream fitness, with studios opening worldwide and celebrities showcasing aerial skills on social media. This transformation represents just the beginning of what's possible for our industry.

The COVID-19 pandemic accelerated changes that were already underway - digital integration, hybrid learning models, and increased focus on mental health benefits alongside physical fitness. Studios that adapted quickly, like we did with the Aerial Education Hub, discovered new revenue streams and deeper student engagement. These innovations aren't temporary pandemic responses - they're permanent shifts that define the future of aerial arts.

Access your free subscripton to Aerial Studio Boost online for free resources

Chapter 15

THE FUTURE OF AERIAL ARTS

Industry Trends and Opportunities

Mainstream Fitness Integration Aerial arts is transitioning from specialty studios to mainstream fitness offerings. Traditional gyms are adding aerial classes, and fitness chains are incorporating aerial elements into their programs. This creates opportunities for experienced instructors and challenges for standalone studios to differentiate themselves.

Wellness and Mental Health Focus The industry is shifting from purely physical fitness to holistic wellness. Students increasingly seek aerial arts for stress relief, confidence building, and mental health benefits. Studios that understand and market these aspects will capture growing demand from wellness-focused consumers.

Corporate and Therapeutic Applications Businesses are discovering aerial arts for team building and employee wellness programs. Healthcare professionals are exploring aerial therapy for rehabilitation and mental health treatment. These emerging markets offer premium pricing and stable revenue streams for studios positioned to serve them.

Inclusive and Adaptive Programming The future belongs to studios that serve diverse populations. Adaptive aerial programs for people with disabilities, senior-friendly classes, and body-positive approaches are expanding the potential student base beyond traditional demographics.

Chapter 15

THE FUTURE OF AERIAL ARTS

Emerging Markets and Niches

Youth and Teen Programs The next generation of aerial artists is starting younger. Youth programs like our ages 8-15 classes represent significant growth opportunities. Parents increasingly seek activities that build confidence, strength, and social skills - aerial arts delivers all three.

Men's Aerial Fitness Male participation in aerial arts is growing as the fitness benefits become more widely recognised. Studios that successfully market to men and create welcoming environments for male students will tap into an underserved market.

Aerial Arts Tourism Destination workshops, aerial retreats, and vacation packages combining travel with intensive training are emerging trends. Studios in attractive locations can develop tourism revenue streams while building international reputations.

Professional Development and Certification As the industry matures, demand for professional training and certification programs increases. Studios with strong reputations can develop instructor training programs, creating high-value revenue streams while contributing to industry standards.

Hybrid Online-Offline Models The future isn't purely digital or purely physical - it's hybrid. Students want flexibility to practice at home and attend studio classes. The Aerial Education Hub model, providing digital content alongside physical classes, represents the direction the industry is moving.

Chapter 15

THE FUTURE OF AERIAL ARTS

Technology Integration Possibilities

Virtual Reality Training VR technology is beginning to enable aerial arts training in virtual environments. While not replacing physical practice, VR can help students visualise sequences, practice choreography, and overcome fear barriers before attempting moves in person.

Wearable Technology Integration Fitness trackers and smart clothing can monitor aerial arts performance, tracking metrics like heart rate, muscle engagement, and movement patterns. This data can inform training programs and demonstrate fitness benefits to students.

AI-Powered Personalisation Artificial intelligence can analyse student progress, suggest appropriate sequences, and customise training programs based on individual goals and abilities. This technology can enhance the personal training experience while reducing instructor workload.

Advanced Booking and Management Systems Future studio management platforms will integrate more deeply with student experiences - predictive scheduling, automated progress tracking, and personalised communication based on behaviour patterns and preferences.

Live Streaming and Remote Instruction High-quality streaming technology enables real-time instruction for students who can't attend physical classes. This technology expands your potential student base beyond geographic limitations while maintaining personal connection

Chapter 15

THE FUTURE OF AERIAL ARTS

Sustainability and Environmental Consciousness

Eco-Friendly Equipment and Practices Environmental consciousness is influencing purchasing decisions across all industries. Studios that prioritise sustainable equipment, energy-efficient facilities, and environmentally responsible practices will appeal to increasingly eco-conscious consumers.

Community Impact Focus Future successful studios will demonstrate clear community impact beyond just fitness services. Programs for underserved populations, mental health support, and community building will become competitive advantages.

The Franchise and Expansion Opportunity

Standardised Systems Enable Growth The aerial arts industry is mature enough for successful franchise models. Studios with proven systems, like the model we're developing at Aerial Arts Academy, can expand rapidly while maintaining quality through standardised training and operations.

International Expansion Aerial arts popularity is growing globally, creating opportunities for international expansion. Studios with strong digital components can serve international markets while building toward physical presence in new countries.

Brand Building and Recognition As the industry grows, brand recognition becomes more valuable. Studios that build strong local reputations can leverage that success for expansion, franchising, or acquisition opportunities.

Chapter 15

THE FUTURE OF AERIAL ARTS

Next Steps for Studio Owners

Assess Your Current Position Evaluate your studio's strengths, weaknesses, and market position. Are you positioned to capitalise on emerging trends? Do your systems support growth? Are you serving current students well enough to expand?

Invest in Technology Infrastructure Ensure your studio has the technology foundation to support future growth. This includes robust booking systems, digital content capabilities, and data analytics to understand student behavior and preferences.

Develop Multiple Revenue Streams Diversify beyond group classes to include private lessons, workshops, online content, corporate programs, and retail opportunities. Multiple revenue streams provide stability and growth potential.

Build Scalable Systems Document your processes, standardise your training, and create systems that can operate without your constant involvement. This foundation enables growth while maintaining quality.

Focus on Community and Culture Technology and systems are important, but community remains the heart of successful studios. Invest in building strong relationships with students, instructors, and your local community.

Stay Connected to Industry Trends Join professional organisations, attend conferences, and network with other studio owners. The aerial arts industry is small enough that sharing knowledge benefits everyone while keeping you informed about emerging opportunities.

Your Future Planning Action Steps

Immediate Actions (Next 30 Days)

- ☐ Assess current technology systems and identify upgrade needs
- ☐ Survey students about interest in new program types or services
- ☐ Research emerging trends in your local market
- ☐ Evaluate your studio's digital presence and online capabilities
- ☐ Review financial performance and identify growth opportunities

Short-term Goals (Next 6 Months)

- ☐ Implement technology upgrades to support future growth
- ☐ Develop at least one new revenue stream or program type
- ☐ Create or improve online content offerings
- ☐ Establish partnerships with complementary businesses
- ☐ Document key processes and systems for scalability

Chapter 15

THE FUTURE OF AERIAL ARTS

Your Future Planning Action Steps

Long-term Vision (Next 2-5 Years)
☐ Develop expansion plans based on market opportunities
☐ Build brand recognition and reputation in your region
☐ Create passive income streams through digital products
☐ Consider franchise or licensing opportunities
☐ Establish your studio as a leader in emerging trends

Ongoing Development
☐ Continuously monitor industry trends and adapt accordingly
☐ Invest in professional development and industry knowledge
☐ Build relationships with other studio owners and industry leaders
☐ Maintain focus on student satisfaction and community building
☐ Regular review and adjustment of business strategy

Your Future Planning Action Steps

The Opportunity Ahead

The aerial arts industry is at an inflection point.

The combination of mainstream acceptance, technological advancement, and growing awareness of mental health benefits creates unprecedented opportunities for studio owners who are prepared to embrace change.

Success in the future aerial arts landscape requires balancing innovation with the fundamental elements that make aerial arts special - personal transformation, supportive community, and the joy of movement. Studios that can integrate new technologies and serve emerging markets while maintaining the human connection that draws people to aerial arts will thrive.

The next decade will separate studios that adapt and grow from those that remain static. The tools, systems, and strategies outlined in this book provide the foundation for building a future-ready aerial arts business. The question isn't whether the industry will continue evolving - it's whether you'll be leading that evolution or struggling to keep up.

Your Future Planning Action Steps

Your Legacy in Aerial Arts

As you build your aerial arts studio, remember that you're not just running a business - you're contributing to an industry that transforms lives. Every student who gains confidence, every instructor who develops their skills, and every community member who discovers the joy of aerial arts is part of your legacy.

The future of aerial arts will be shaped by studio owners who combine business acumen with genuine passion for the art form. Those who invest in their students, support their instructors, and contribute to the broader aerial arts community will build businesses that thrive while making meaningful impacts.

Your studio has the potential to be more than a fitness business - it can be a catalyst for personal transformation, a hub for community building, and a leader in an industry that's just beginning to realise its potential.

The future is bright for aerial arts, and studio owners who are prepared to embrace that future will find opportunities beyond what we can imagine today.

Your Future Planning Action Steps

Final Thoughts

The journey of building a successful aerial arts studio is challenging, rewarding, and never truly finished. As you implement the strategies and systems outlined in this book, remember that every expert was once a beginner. Your passion for aerial arts, combined with proven business principles, can create something extraordinary.

The aerial arts community is waiting for what you'll build...

Resources & Recommended Tools

The right tools can transform your studio operations from chaotic to systematic. Here are the platforms and services that have proven essential for building and scaling Aerial Arts Academy.

Learning Resources

Aerial Education Hub: aerial-education-hub.circle.so (as a Kindle book purchaser you get 50% discount on the platform. Use code **KBP50OFF**

Aerial Studio Boost: https://aerial-studio-boost.circle.s (as a Kindle book purchaser you get 50% discount on the platform. Use code **KBP50OFF**

Essential Studio Management

Go Team Up - Studio Management Platform

Website: https://goteamup.com/

What it does: Comprehensive studio management solution handling booking, payments, membership management, and communication

Why we recommend it: This is the backbone of our entire operation. Go Team Up manages everything from class scheduling across multiple venues to automated billing and customer communication.

Key features: Online booking, GoCardless, Paypal and Stripe payment integration, membership tiers, automated emails, waitlists, reporting, mobile app and much MORE!

Best for: Studios of all sizes looking for an all-in-one solution

Getting started: Start with their free trial and configure your class schedule, pricing, and basic policies before going live

Resources & Recommended Tools

Brevo - CRM & Marketing Platform

Website: https://www.brevo.com

What it does: Comprehensive CRM and marketing automation

Why mentioned: Suitable for larger operations needing advanced customer relationship management. But great for small businesses too as they have a low cost entry version.

Best for: Established studios with complex marketing needs and larger customer bases

Social Media Management

Social Pilot - Social Media Scheduling

Website: https://www.socialpilot.co/

What it does: Schedule and manage social media posts across multiple platforms

Why we recommend it: Saves hours of manual posting while maintaining consistent social media presence

Key features: Content scheduling, team collaboration, analytics, bulk uploading

Best for: Studios wanting to maintain regular social media presence efficiently

Getting started: Set up content calendars for your key platforms and batch-create posts weekly

Resources & Recommended Tools

Insurance & Risk Management

Insure4Sport - Specialised Fitness Insurance

Website: www.insure4sport.co.uk/RAF312

What it does: Insurance specifically designed for fitness and aerial arts businesses

Why we strongly recommend it: Essential protection for aerial arts studios. They understand the unique risks of our industry.

Key coverage: Public liability, professional indemnity, equipment cover, business interruption

Best for: All aerial arts studios - this is non-negotiable protection
Getting started: Get quotes for your specific activities and venue arrangements

Financial Management

Xero - Accounting Software

Website: https://www.xero.com/

What it does: Cloud-based accounting and financial management
Why we recommend it: Integrates well with other platforms and provides clear financial reporting

Key features: Invoicing, expense tracking, bank reconciliation, financial reporting, tax preparation

Best for: Studios needing professional financial management and reporting

Getting started: Connect your business bank account and set up your chart of accounts

159

Resources & Recommended Tools

Stripe / PayPal - Payment Processing

Website: www.paypal.com/ or **https://stripe.com/**

What it does: Online payment processing for businesses

Why mentioned: Integrates seamlessly with Go Team Up for membership and class payments

Key features: Secure payment processing, subscription billing, international payments

Best for: Any studio taking online payments

Note: Usually set up automatically through your booking system

Automation & Integration

Zapier - Workflow Automation

Website: https://zapier.com/

What it does: Connects different apps and automates workflows between them

Why we recommend it: Eliminates manual data entry and creates seamless connections between your tools

Key features: Automated workflows, data synchronisation, trigger-based actions

Best for: Studios using multiple platforms that need to work together

Getting started: Start with simple automations like adding new Go Team Up members to your Brevo email list

Resources & Recommended Tools

Professional Development & Training

Spin City - Teacher Training

Website: https://spincity.co.uk/

What it does: Professional pole dance and aerial instructor training and certification

Why we recommend as the top choice: Quality training provider for instructor development. Both online and offline courses at affordable prices. Recognised qualification provider that meets our instructor standards at Aerial Arts Academy - our go to provider!

Best for: Studios needing qualified pole dance and aerial instructors who want qualifications with international recognition

<u>Use code NSCA20 for 20% OFF</u>

Xpert - Pole & Aerial Training

Website: https://xpertpole.com/

What it does: Comprehensive pole dance and aerial arts instructor training and certification

Key features: Pole dance instructor courses, aerial training, continuing education

Best for: Instructors seeking professional qualifications and studios building qualified teaching teams

Resources & Recommended Tools

IPDFA - International Pole Dance Fitness Association

Website: https://ipdfa.com/

What it does: Professional pole dance instructor certification and continuing education

Best for: Instructors seeking internationally recognised qualifications

Equipment & Safety Resources

Aerial Studio Boost - Professional Pole / Aerial Equipment

Website: www.aerialstudioboost.com

What it does: Premium aerial and pole dance equipment supplier

Why we recommend it: Renowned for top-tier quality and reliability, their competition poles and aerial arts equipment are professional-grade and trusted by studios globally.

Key products: Static and spinning poles, portable and permanent installations, accessories, mats, aerial kits, silks, hoops - everything you need in one place

Best for: Studios wanting professional-grade aerial equipment. Also the place for studio owners to go to for online business and marketing support.

Access your free subscripton to Aerial Studio Boost online for free resources

Resources & Recommended Tools

Firetoys - Aerial Arts Equipment Supplier

Website: https://www.firetoys.com/

What it does: supplier of aerial arts equipment, rigging hardware, and safety gear

Why we recommend it: Trusted UK supplier

Key products: Aerial silks, hoops, rigging points, safety equipment, mats, and accessories

Best for: Studios needing reliable aerial equipment and rigging supplies

Getting started: Consult with their rigging experts for safe installation and equipment selection

Professional Rigging Services

What you need: Certified riggers for safe aerial point installation.

Key rigging contact trusted by Aerial Arts Academy:

Oliver Ward. Director UKCF. enquiries@oliverward.co.uk
+44 7915818006

Key considerations: Structural assessments, safety certifications

Safety note: Never attempt rigging installation without professional expertise - safety is non-negotiable

Resources & Recommended Tools

NewtonsLadder

Website: https://www.newtonsladder.co.uk

What it does: Professional rigging and structural engineering services for aerial arts installations

Why we recommend it: Specialised expertise in aerial arts rigging with proper structural assessments and safety certifications

Key services: Structural surveys, rigging point installation, safety inspections, load calculations

Best for: Studios needing professional rigging installation and safety assessments

Getting started: Contact them for a structural assessment before any aerial point installation

Anptrussing

If you are looking for a truss system contact anptrussing for state of the art black truss system to hire for your pole/aerial events

Instagram [@undefined]

Instagram photos and videos

instagram

Resources & Recommended Tools

Getting Started Recommendations

For New Studios (0-50 members):

1. Go Team Up - Essential for professional operations from day one

2. Insure4Sport - Non-negotiable protection

3. Brevo - Start building your email list immediately

4. Basic social media - Focus on one platform initially

5. Rigging - Professional rigging assessment and installation

For Growing Studios (50-150 members):

1. Add Social Pilot for a consistent social media presence

2. Implement Xero for professional financial management

3. Set up Zapier automations to reduce manual work

4. Invest in instructor training and development

For Established Studios (150+ members):

1. Consider HubSpot for advanced customer relationship management

2. Develop comprehensive staff training programs

3. Explore franchise or expansion opportunities

4. Build strategic partnerships with complementary businesses

Resources & Recommended Tools

Implementation Tips

Start Simple: Don't try to implement everything at once. Begin with Go Team Up and insurance, then add tools as you grow.

Integration First: Choose tools that work well together. The Go Team Up + Brevo + Social Pilot combination is proven to work seamlessly.

Training Investment: Budget for proper training on each platform. The time invested in learning these tools properly pays dividends in efficiency.

Regular Reviews: Assess your tools quarterly. As your studio grows, your needs may change, and new solutions may become available.

Support Matters: Choose providers with good customer support. When you have technical issues, quick resolution is crucial for studio operations.

Resources & Recommended Tools

Free Resources

Social Media Templates

- Many platforms offer free content templates
- Canva provides aerial arts-specific design templates
- Buffer offers free social media planning tools

Go Team Up Resources

- Free trial period to test all features
- Comprehensive setup guides and video tutorials
- Regular webinars on best practices

Brevo Free Plan

- Up to 300 emails per day for free
- Basic automation features
- Perfect for testing email marketing

The right tools don't just make your life easier - they make your studio more professional, your students happier, and your business more profitable. Start with the essentials and build your toolkit as you grow.

Resources & Recommended Tools

BookWhen - Alternative Booking System

Website: https://bookwhen.com/

What it does: Online booking and payment system

Why mentioned: Previously used system that works well for smaller operations

Best for: Studios just starting out or those needing simpler booking functionality

Email Marketing & Communication

Brevo (formerly Sendinblue)

Website: https://www.brevo.com/

What it does: Email marketing platform with automation capabilities

Why we recommend it: Perfect for studios wanting professional email marketing without enterprise costs. Integrates well with Go Team Up for segmented campaigns.

Key features: Automated email sequences, newsletter campaigns, contact segmentation, A/B testing

Best for: Studios ready to implement systematic email marketing

Getting started: Begin with welcome sequences for new members and monthly newsletters

I want to express my heartfelt gratitude to the Aerial Arts Academy team for their contributions and for allowing us to use their photography, including Ellie Green Photography. The remarkable AAA team is the driving force behind our existence, keeping our vibrant community thriving—thank you all!

I hope this resource has been helpful to you. If you need further assistance, join us on Aerial Studio Boost online and chat with me live!

Warm regards,
Nicola Ghalmi

Contact Information

↘ **Website:**

www.aerialstudioboost.com

↘ **Email:**

info@aerialstudioboost.com

www.ingramcontent.com/pod-product-compliance
Lightning Source LLC
Chambersburg PA
CBHW041216220326
41597CB00033BA/5983